The economic development of Japan 1868–1941

New Studies in Economic and Social History

Edited for the Economic History Society by
Michael Sanderson
University of East Anglia, Norwich

This series, specially commissioned by the Economic History Society, provides a guide to the current interpretations of the key themes of economic and social history in which advances have recently been made or in which there has been significant debate.

In recent times economic and social history has been one of the most flourishing areas of historical study. This has mirrored the increasing relevance of the economic and social sciences both in a student's choice of career and in forming a society at large more aware of the importance of these issues in their everyday lives. Moreover specialist interests in business, agricultural and welfare history, for example, have themselves burgeoned and there has been an increased interest in the economic development of the wider world. Stimulating as these scholarly developments have been for the specialist, the rapid advance of the subject and the quantity of new publications make it difficult for the reader to gain an overview of particular topics, let alone the whole field.

New Studies in Economic and Social History is intended for students and their teachers. It is designed to introduce them to fresh topics and to enable them to keep abreast of recent writing and debates. All the books in the series are written by a recognised authority in the subject, and the arguments and issues are set out in a critical but unpartisan fashion. The aim of the series is to survey the current state of scholarship, rather than to provide a set of prepackaged conclusions.

The series has been edited since its inception in 1968 by Professors M. W. Flinn, T. C. Smout and L. A. Clarkson, and is currently edited by Dr Michael Sanderson. From 1968 it was published by Macmillan as *Studies in Economic History*, and after 1974 as *Studies in Economic and Social History*. From 1995 *New Studies in Economic and Social History* is being published on behalf of the Economic History Society by Cambridge University Press. This new series includes some of the titles previously published by Macmillan as well as new titles, and reflects the ongoing development throughout the world of this rich seam of history.

For a full list of titles in print, please see the end of the book.

The economic development of Japan 1868–1941

Prepared for the Economic History Society by

W. J. Macpherson
University of East Cambridge

CAMBRIDGE
UNIVERSITY PRESS

Published by the Press Syndicate of the University of Cambridge
The Pitt Building, Trumpington Street, Cambridge CB2 1RP
40 West 20th Street, New York, NY 10011-4211, USA
10 Stamford Road, Oakleigh, Melbourne 3166, Australia

The Economic Development of Japan c. 1868–1941 was first published by
The Macmillan Press Limited 1987
First Cambridge University Press edition 1995

Printed in Great Britain at the University Press, Cambridge

A catalogue record for this book is available from the British Library

Library of Congress cataloguing in publication data

Macpherson, W. J.
   The economic development of Japan 1868–1941.
      p.   cm. – (New studies in economic and social history)
   Includes bibliographical references and index.
   ISBN 0 521 55261 3 (hc). – ISBN 0 521 55792 5 (pb)
   1. Japan – Economic conditions – 1868–1918. 2. Japan – Economic
conditions – 1918–1945. I. Title. II. Series.
HC462.7.M25   1995   95–18743
338.952–dc20   CIP

ISBN 0 521 55261 3 hardback
ISBN 0 521 55792 5 paperback

CE

Contents

List of tables

Note on references

References in the text within square brackets relate to the numbered items in the Bibliography; followed, where necessary, by the page numbers in italics, for example [1, 7–9].

Preface

An attempt to describe and evaluate Japanese economic development in so short a space may seem bold and even foolhardy. Much statistical evidence has had to be condensed and analysis of complex issues distilled to the bare essence. Constraints on the size of the bibliography prevented due acknowledgement of the multitude of authorities to whom the author is indebted, as he is to his family for practical help and encouragement. Particular thanks are due to the present and previous editors of the series for their patience and to an anonymous reader for his invaluable suggestions. It is hoped that at least non-specialists will be motivated to read further about one of the most remarkable economic histories of the twentieth century.

Grateful acknowledgement is made for permission to reprint the tables from K. Ohkawa and M. Shinohara with Larry Meissner (eds), *Patterns of Japanese Economic Development. A Quantitative Appraisal*, to the authors and to Yale University.

1
Introduction

In the middle of the nineteenth century the first British Minister to Japan described it as 'a cluster of islands on the furthest edge of the horizon, inhabited by a race grotesque and savage'. In the last quarter of the twentieth century Japan is the world's third largest industrial power [4; 100]. In the 1960s the average annual compound rate of growth of real GNP was nearly 12 per cent and of GNP per head of total population nearly 11 per cent [114, 25]. This post-war 'economic miracle' was regarded with a mixture of awe and alarm by some western observers and occasioned a flood of books with titles such as *How Japan's Economy Grew So Fast* [27], *Asia's New Giant* [126], *Japan as Number One* [169], and *The Emerging Japanese Superstate* [69]. The social costs of rapid growth have resulted in some tempering of earlier euphoria. The inverted commas in the title of Morishima's *Why has Japan 'Succeeded'?* [89] are not fortuitous. Ohkawa and Rosovsky rightly warn against the temptation to 'accentuate the positive' to the neglect of the 'darker side' [114, *228*; 6; 90; 147].

There is a variety of interpretations of post-Second World War growth but two things are certain. The first is the truism that growth is a function of a large number of interacting variables, climatological, geographical, religious, sociological, political, as well as economic, many of which are not conducive to quantification. The second is that growth in any period has its roots in earlier periods. The Second World War marked a transition, some would say, from monarchical absolutism to bourgeois republicanism with only a 'symbolic' emperor, but the pace and character of recent events were influenced by changes dating back to the Meiji Restoration and even to the preceding Tokugawa era. Rostow gives the 'tentative, approximate' dates for Japanese 'take-off' as 1878–1900 [137, *38;* 138]. Kuznets dates the beginning of 'modern economic growth' in 1874–9 [77, *24*], and Rosovsky in 1886 [135, *92*]. How one dates and what one means by the 'beginnings of modern growth' are matters for discussion. What is important is that although there was acceleration after the Second World War, the average annual rate of increase of real GNP between 1901 and 1937 at 3.75 per cent was spectacular enough to merit a thorough examination of the years before Pearl Harbour.

This examination is facilitated by the comparative richness of the raw and processed evidence readily accessible in Japanese and even in English. However, apart altogether from the ideological bias which influences even the most detached scholar, there are problems of data, regions, time and people. The volumes on the *Estimates of Long-Term Economic Statistics of Japan since 1868 (LTES)* [117] provide data on economic indicators of a comprehensiveness unusual in most countries. Nonetheless there are doubts about early Meiji figures and speculation about the Tokugawa era. The plethora of statistics and their increasing manipulation by econometric historians should not blind one to the existence of large margins of error.

All-Japan generalisations mask considerable diversity in climate, topography and regions, and in economic activity and performance. In the Tokugawa period, there was relatively fast economic advance in some areas and regionally varied demographic change. Today, modern industry is heavily concentrated in the 'Tokaido belt' which produces three-quarters of manufactured output, employs 80 per cent of factory workers and suffers external diseconomies such as land scarcity, excess density, traffic jams and pollution. In agriculture the typology rightly stresses the universality of small, rice-growing farms, but the northern island of Hokkaido contrasts markedly with southern regions in crops, output, size of farm, land-use rate and weather. Indeed, farming in Eastern Hokkaido has a West European rather than a Japanese appearance. One could follow the geographers along the alluvial plains and irrigated paddy fields through suburban horticulture with back-pack technology to the wheat-growing uplands, to provide a picture of infinite complexity.

Regional income disparities have occasioned growing concern to recent governments. In 1959 average per capita income in Tokyo-to was 63 per cent above the national average; in Kagoshima-ken it was 40 per cent below [172]. Umemura found a regional relation between income and occupational distribution [166]. In 1960 annual average income in Southern Kyushu with 54 per cent of employment in the primary sector was only about 60 per cent of all-Japan income. Of course, data of the above sort present serious problems of definition and compilation and the regional picture was not static. The general message remains, that macro studies and national aggregates conceal spatial divergences.

There also have been chronological fluctuations, some due to natural disasters such as typhoons, floods, volcanic eruptions and the Great Kanto earthquake of 1923. In addition the Second World War interrupted the growth trend with real GNP in 1946 marginally below the 1918 level and only about half of the 1937 level. It was probably not until 1952 that the 1937 GNP level was again reached. By contrast Japan was only peripherally involved in the 1914–18 war, was able to take advantage of the dislocation in other countries, and achieved rapid growth of exports and increased shipping earnings which transformed the persistent current account balance of payment deficits of the period 1903–14 into large surpluses during the war. Sensitivity to external events was again demonstrated in the world depression with a halving of the value of the main export, silk, between 1920 and 1930. The ensuing peasant distress, widespread unemployment, growing economic nationalism abroad and alleged Chinese threats to Manchuria contributed to changes in economic policy, the collapse of parliamentary 'democracy' and the rise of rightist militarism.

Attempts to identify and measure periodisation in Japanese economic growth raise problems over indicators, base years, turning points and the different experience of the agrarian and non-agrarian sectors. Central to the work of Ohkawa and Rosovsky [114] are periods of relatively faster and slower growth within an accelerating trend. Long swings have been an enduring feature and closely related, statistically and causally, with private and total capital formation. Upswings are characterised by 'investment spurts' and downswings by slower investment growth. The existence of long swings has been confirmed more recently by Ohkawa in Ohkawa and Shinohara [116] with four upswings and three downswings from the 1880s to the 1960s. (See Table 1 below.) Oscillations in growth are not peculiar to Japan. What is unusual is that each upswing had a faster rate of growth than its predecessor.

Another significant and complex issue is the behaviour and attitudes of the Japanese people, and the 'national ethos'. These were a determinant of the growth and structure of the economy and, in turn, were influenced by economic change.

The Japanese may have had mixed Ainu, Malay and Mongol origins but remoteness and isolation developed exclusiveness, uniformity and remarkable homogeneity of language and culture. In addition the coexistence of traditional and modern elements [130] and the peculiar nature of this society have confounded facile attempts to fit it into general western theories such as those of Maine or Marx or Weber. Certainly one can see elements of movements from status to contract, from feudalism to capitalism and also the influence of a religious ethic. But Japanese frugality was hardly Calvinistic, its 'capitalism' was idiosyncratic and the Confucianism and Taoism imported from China underwent a drastic sea-change. These singularities have not only stimulated much sociological debate but have also queried the relevance of the Japanese experience as a model for LDCs and the viability of importing Japanese labour practices to British and American car plants [19].

Among the features of society most commented upon were discipline, a clear concept of and acceptance of authority, loyalty and deference to superiors and an emphasis on birth and seniority rather than on merit. Most important was the subjection of individualism to the group, originally the *ie* or household later transferred to the company or firm. This 'groupism' appears in the loyalty of workers to a paternalistic company rather than to craft and industrial workers in other enterprises, and in the participation of company employees in group decision-making. Before the Second World War, the Government encouraged through the educational system and State Shinto, a belief in the emperor as a symbol of Japan's divine origins and destined greatness. Some of these 'traditional' features were compared unfavourably as distortions, with an idealised model of western industrial society. They were seen both as evidence of Japan's lagging development or unripe capitalism and as inhibitors of 'modernisation'. More recently, sociologists are more concerned with the positive effects on industrialisation of Japan's social structure and attitudes and are evaluating the lessons they contain for the West.

While Japanese society has enough common characteristics to make some generalisation meaningful, even the casual observer is as much struck by paradoxes and contradictions as by homogeneity. The subservience of the Japanese did not prevent frequent peasant revolts and the rice riots of 1918 [13]. The Meiji Restoration was less bloody than some revolutions but there were rebellions, notably the Satsuma uprising in 1877. Neither the structure of society nor its attitudes were constant. They were moulded and altered by economic forces. The lowly-ranked merchants in the Tokugawa hierarchy became a powerful group long before 1868. The twentieth-century witnesses, in Dore's words [29, 4] 'a movement towards greater flexibility, greater individuation and greater rationality'. In another context Dore's 'good' Meiji landlords became the parasites of the 1920s. Vogel [168, 86] doubts whether the nationalist doctrines of the 1930s were ever fully 'internalised' by his salaried men. The famous Japanese industrial relations system with its employer paternalism, reciprocal loyalties, lifetime commitment and seniority wages, developed and adapted alongside modern industry. Its origins lie at least as much in the economic realities of labour market problems as in sociological paternalism or dynastic élitism. Nor was it typical outside the male workforce in the modern factory sector. In 1930 over half of the workers in factories with five or more employees were women. In cotton textiles females comprised about 80 per cent of the workforce [160, 98]. Women workers experienced different systems of recruitment, were much more transient and earned less than their male counterparts. There is a growing literature not only on women [133; 146] but also about disadvantaged minorities such as the Ainu, the Buraku, the Koreans and Okinawans, to whom the benefits of growth have not fully 'trickled-down' [170].

Ideological bias, inadequate data, spatial and temporal dissimilarities and the existence of social and economic minorities provide the complex reality behind general statements and theses about 'the Japanese' and 'Japanese economic growth'. They explain the large number of different methods and schools and interpretations of historical change [57]. Japan has been described

as 'a battle ground for competing theories and economic development' and as a testing ground for 'labour-surplus' and neoclassical
models [26; 71; 113; 118]. The English-language literature has
been dominated by Americans and 'modernisation theory', critical
of the Marxist orientation of much of the Japanese literature [22;
33; 65]. The Marxists themselves divided into the *Rōnōha* school
who argued that the Meiji Restoration was essentially a bourgeois
revolution leading to a modern industrial capitalist society and the
Kōzaha who stressed absolute monarchism and the persistence of
feudal remnants [157]. Disenchantment with all these and concern
for 'the people' (*Minshū*), has spawned 'people's histories' (*Min-
shūshi*), about village daily life and customs, popular rights movements and ethnography in general [38]. The careful scholar should
apply to all this historiography the same spirit of critical eclecticism
which the Japanese themselves demonstrated in their attempts to
catch up with the West.

2
Growth and structural change

Kuznets identified the economic growth of nations as 'a sustained increase in per capita or per worker product, mostly often accompanied by an increase in population and usually by sweeping structural changes'. Of course, 'growthmania' may neglect distribution, basic needs, social indicators, equality and strategies which are less oriented to maximising output growth. In Japan material progress was historically related to political and social costs, most strikingly in the case of militarism.

Table 1, overleaf [116, *10*] illustrates the general growth picture and its fluctuations.

Japan was already relatively densely populated in 1868 but it is clear from Table 1 that population growth has been moderate, nearer to British rates during the Industrial Revolution than to the much higher rates in many LDCs since the Second World War. The upswings, downswings and trend acceleration in economic growth, already noted, are prominent. In the past decade or so rates of growth have been slower, raising the possibility that there is now a phase of trend deceleration. Japan started her modern economic growth at a much lower level of per capita income than did most other now developed countries. Even in 1974 the UN International Comparison Project [76] found that GDP per capita was only 63 per cent of that in the USA and below that in most industrialised societies except the UK and Italy. But the gap has been steadily narrowing over time. Only the USA among 14 non-socialist countries had a historically faster rate of growth of total product and Sweden of per capita. The Japanese record is particularly striking in the pre-war Asian context. British India between 1858 and 1947 achieved an average per annum total GDP growth rate of

Table 1 *Long-term pattern of aggregate growth rates, constant price series: average annual growth rates. (in percent)*

Period (length in years)	Gross National Expenditure	Total population	Per capita GNE	Personal consumption Total	Personal consumption Per capita[a]	Personal consumption Difference from per capita GNE[b]
A. Long-swing phases						
(U) 1887–97 (10)	3.21	0.96	2.25	3.15	2.19	−0.06
(D) 1897–1904 (7)	1.83	1.16	0.67	1.02	−0.14	−0.81
(U) 1904–19 (15)	3.30	1.19	2.11	2.99	1.80	−0.31
(D) 1919–30 (11)	2.40	1.51	0.89	2.60	1.09	0.20
(U) 1930–38 (8)	4.88	1.28	2.60	2.23	0.95	−2.65
(D) 1938–53 (15)	0.58	1.36	−0.78	0.89	−0.47	0.31
(D) 1953–69 (16)	9.56	1.03	8.53	8.63	7.60	−0.93
B. Trough-to-trough and peak-to-peak						
(T) 1887–1904 (17)	2.64	1.04	1.60	2.27	1.23	−0.37
(P) 1897–1919 (22)	2.72	1.18	1.54	2.37	1.09	−0.54
(T) 1904–30 (26)	2.92	1.32	1.60	2.83	1.51	−0.09
(P) 1919–38 (19)	3.44	1.35	2.09	2.44	1.09	−1.00
(T) 1930–53 (23)	2.08	1.29	0.79	1.36	0.07	−0.72
(P) 1938–69 (31)	5.21	1.06	4.16	4.51	3.45	−0.71
C. Secular trends						
1887–1930 (43)	2.81	1.21	1.60	2.61	1.40	−0.20
1904–38 (34)	3.26	1.25	2.01	2.69	1.44	−0.57
1887–1938 (51)	3.13	1.22	1.91	2.55	1.33	−0.58
1887–1969 (82)	3.92	1.21	2.71	3.29	2.08	−0.63
1904–69 (65)	4.19	1.17	3.02	3.55	2.38	−0.64

Notes: Annual growth rates are calculated as a percentage increase from the preceding year, then a period average growth rate is taken as the simple average of the individual years' growth rates, except that 1938–53 is a simple bridge between the two years because of the lack of consistent data. Turning points are based on GNP; 1887, 1953 and 1969 are tentative. The series are smoothed. U = upswing; D = downswing; P = peak; T = trough.

[a] Personal consumption's growth rate minus that of total population.

[b] Per capita personal consumption's growth rate minus that of per capita GNE.

only about 1 per cent. Interwar Indian output growth was barely sufficient to outstrip population [84, *134*].

A country may achieve fast rates of output growth, but without diversification and structural change it cannot be said to be 'developed'. The Japanese experience exhibits a relative shift from agriculture to manufacturing and from pre-modern to modern industry, but there was also a remarkable persistence of the traditional and small-scale sectors. This persistence has promoted descriptions such as dualistic, differentiated and hybrid and, in particular, a large and controversial literature on the relevance of theories of dualistic development, the role of unlimited supplies of labour and a supposed turning point from labour-surplus to labour-scarcity conditions.

The conventional structural switch is empirically illustrated by differential sectoral growth rates, by the changing share of sectors in GNP and occupations, by alterations in export composition and by variation in manufacturing product. The fastest growth rate was in manufacturing, followed by services and agriculture [101]. From 1887 to 1938 industrial growth (manufacturing, facilitating industries and construction) averaged 6.34 per cent per annum, services 2.60 per cent and agriculture 1.36 per cent [116, *38*]. Oshima [124] gives annual average growth rates of total factor productivity for non-agriculture at 1.1 per cent (1908–38) and 5.7 per cent (1955–70); for agriculture, 0.6 per cent (1901–37) and 2.6 per cent (1955–70). The share of industry in NDP at current prices increased from 20 per cent around 1887 to 51.7 per cent around 1938. The share of services declined from 37.5 to 30 per cent and agriculture even more from 42.5 to 18.5 per cent.

Statements about occupational switches are hazardous in a country where there were so many family enterprises, overlapping of jobs and bye-employment. Farmers, for example, had side-occupations, not only in forestry, fishing and silk-reeling but also in mining, building, transport and communications [127]. Part-time farmers as a percentage of total farmers increased from 55 per cent in 1938 to 78.5 per cent in 1965 [112, *252*]. In the early Meiji period one-third of all the gainfully occupied persons in the two prefectures of Yamanashi and Yamagata had side-jobs [112, *191*]. In the Northern Kyushu coal-districts farmers turned to mining in off-peak periods [104, *24*]. In 1878 the percentage of total occupied population in primary industry was 83.5 (15.7 millions), in secondary industry 5 (925,000) and in tertiary 11.5 (2.1 millions). In 1940 the figures are 44 (14.4 millions), 23.5 (7.6 millions) and 32 (10.4 millions) [109, *145*]. While these crude data evince structural change, they also confirm the endurance of agriculture as an employment source. There is a marked contrast, for example, with Britain, where the percentage of the total occupied population in agriculture was already only 36 in 1801 and 8 in 1911. The existence until recently of a huge reserve army in the rural sector has important connotations for studies of sources of growth and for theories of the dual economy.

Structural change is also evident in the pattern of exports, particularly significant in view of the current concern in some Third World countries about overspecialisation in primary commodities. Matsukata in 1874 was warning against Japan's becoming a mere supplier of primary products [153, *30*]. Japan's early export mix was heavily dominated by agricultural and processed goods, but textiles and more sophisticated manufactures eventually took over. Thus, in 1874–83 in current prices, 42.5 per cent of exports were primary products and 57.5 per cent manufactures. Of the latter, some 42 per cent were textiles, mainly silk. Silk here means raw silk, often categorised as a primary rather than a secondary product. Raw silk dominated Japan's early exports with a share of total merchandise exports ranging from 60 per cent at the Restoration to 46 per cent in the early 1920s. By 1931–40 the share of primary products had fallen to 6.9 per cent with an increase in manufactures to over 93.1 per cent. Most striking is the rise in so-called 'heavy manufactures' as a percentage of exports, from 8.2 in 1874–83 to 28.7 in 1931–40 and to 68.2 in 1966–70 [116, *135*]. Since the Second World War, Japan's outstanding international competitiveness is partly explained by an ability, fostered by state agencies such as the Ministry of Finance and the Ministry of International Trade and Industry, to make structural adjustments in exports, from labour-intensive textiles to capital-intensive ships and steel to sophisticated consumer durables such as cars and televisions and, most recently, to knowledge-intensive industrial machinery and information electronics [32; 85].

Until the 1930s manufacturing output was dominated by foodstuffs such as bean paste, soy sauce and sake, and textiles, especially silk and cotton. 'Heavy' industry had a smaller, but growing share. The dramatic rise in heavy industry was mainly a feature of the 1930s, associated both with industrial maturity and military requirements. In 1885 heavy industry comprised only 16.7 per cent of manufacturing output, food products 42.5 per cent and textiles 29.1 per cent. By 1940, however, the ratio of heavy industry had risen to 58.8 per cent while food products and textiles had fallen to 12.2 and 16.8 per cent, respectively. Other products such as timber, printing and publishing, ceramics and glass were relatively unimportant. It is often alleged that the pattern of industrialisation in 'follower' Japan was essentially unlike that in the first industrial nation. Norman [106, *126*] opined that the 'normal order of transition from light to heavy industry was reversed in Japan'. In his attempt to apply Gerschenkron's theory of relative backwardness Inkster [61, *63*] also stresses 'the disproportionate size of the capital goods industries and heavy industry generally'. Japan was a late-starter, subjected to the tensions of the western impact, for a brief period short of suitably skilled labour and industrial entrepreneurs and reliant to a greater extent than Britain on state capitalism, especially for investment in infrastructure [62]. However, at the end of the nineteenth century, as a percentage of manufacturing output at current prices, machinery comprised only 2.8 and iron and steel 0.54. Japan's early modern industrial structure was markedly biased, not to capital goods, but to 'light' consumer goods, especially processed food and silk and cotton.

Many consumer goods were suitable for a relatively small scale of production unit. One of the most discussed features of Japanese industrialisation is the co-existence of large, capital-intensive, high wage and productivity firms, often using imported technology, and small-medium enterprises relatively labour-intensive with lower wages and productivity. Japan was not unique in the existence of small enterprises [8, *202*] but such dubious comparative data as are available point to a peculiarity in structure. Broadbridge [15, *50*] maintains that in 1960, 15 per cent of Japanese manufacturing workers were in plants employing 1–9 workers, 28 per cent in the 10–49 group and 11 per cent in the 55–99 group. Roughly comparable data for the USA (1958) give 4, 14 and 10; for the UK

(1951) 4, 11 and 10. Shinohara [143] confirms the endurance of the small-medium sector.

Overseas demand was significant for many small industry products such as silk, a classic example of a labour-intensive commodity in family production with a negligible import content. To western schoolboys, metal toys were better known. German toymakers were imitated in the 1880s and the domestic market dominated until 1914. The disruption of German trade after 1914, in toys as in other fields, allowed enterprising Japanese merchants to penetrate overseas markets, and export expanded to a peak in 1937.

Metal toys not only illustrate a characteristic pattern of development from foreign imitation, through the home market to export; they also show in down-town Tokyo, parent assembling factories, mould manufacturers and subcontracted part-makers who, in turn, put out some operations to household workers. Over time experts have been increasingly concentrated in large manufacturing firms, recently in multinationals. However, in 1935 small manufacturing firms produced 65 per cent of manufactured exports and in 1956, 60 per cent [125, *202*]. What the small industries lacked in standardised quality, marketing economies and overseas know-how was partly compensated for by the low prices stemming from cut-throat competition and low labour costs.

For most small-industry products, the home market was the mainstay. Consumption expenditure was dominated by food which accounted for 60 to 65 per cent of the total until 1920 and still about 50 per cent in the 1930s. Clothing's share increased from around 8 per cent in 1880 to 13 per cent in 1940. Most food was the output of the small-scale sector and, despite the expansion of large textile factories, it was also prominent in clothing. Two of the most noted features of Japanese personal expenditure are a surprisingly low marginal propensity to consume and high savings rate and the persistence of traditional consumption patterns until post-Second World War. This persistence was a function of both relatively low incomes, by western standards, and inherited social attitudes to wants.

On the supply side small industries suffered from a relatively high supply price of external finance. But many were 'profitable' and had a high propensity to replough profits. In 1957 plants with less than 10 workers had wages only 60 per cent of the national average and a capital–labour ratio of only 24 per cent [114, 51]. Second-hand technology, although sometimes causing maintenance and spare-part problems, economised on fixed capital. The Prince of Satsuma purchased second-hand ships from Britain, Holland and Germany. The proportion of second-hand machinery to total fixed investment in 1957 was 41 per cent in factories with 4–9 employees compared with 3.3 per cent in those in the 1000-plus group.

As in eighteenth-century Britain, technical progress was partly the result of small-scale changes arising from practical experimentation and learning by doing, but the dramatic breakthroughs now discounted in the British experience were much more impressive in late-starting Japan. For example, in a few decades water wheels were displaced by steam engines and then by thermal and hydro-electric power. By 1905 the horsepower generated by electric motors exceeded that by water-wheels and by 1917 that by steam engines. The percentage of electric motors in prime movers in establishments employing 5–9 workers increased from 17 in 1909 to 92 in 1930 and to 95 in 1940, by which time the ratio was not much below that in the 1000-plus worker group. Electric motors were efficient, easily adaptable to small units and relatively cheap. Electrification benefited from externalities caused by complementary developments in utilities and the electrical machine industry. Technical progress of this kind reduced productivity differentials by scale and, coupled with low wages, ensured the profitability of small businesses, ameliorating the labour absorption problem of the 1920s when both agriculture and the large-scale sector were dispensing with surplus workers. Motive power is a classic case of Japanese technological innovation, in the early stages reliant on eclectic borrowing from Britain, France, Germany and the United States, demonstrating adaptability to factor endowments by ingenious manufacturers and resulting eventually in a large domestic supplying industry, independent of imports. The speed of what Inkster [61] calls this technical 'contagion' was highlighted by Minami [125, 299]. He hypothesises that if steam technology had persisted as long in Japan as in the 'earlier developed' countries, smaller enterprises would have been 'swept away'.

Much Japanese research relates to *chusho kigyo mondai*, that is 'small and medium enterprises as a social problem' [48, *225*; 157, *324*]. Small firms exploited cheap migrant labour supplied by farmer agrarian quasi-serfs and, in turn, were exploited by mono-poly capital which grew 'as a risk-free parasite'. Morishima [89, *110*] believes that the wage disparity between large and small enterprises developed into 'a chronic illness of the Japanese economy'. Although Caves and Uekusa [18] question the distinc-tiveness of the Japanese institution and do not regard it as abnormal in view of the country's size, income level and speed of growth, they agree that factor-price distortions explain its techni-ques. The *bête noire* in most of the criticisms is the subcontracting system.

Even very small firms undertake some subcontracting but it is most significant in large enterprises. In 1973, for example, over 83 per cent of Japanese manufacturing establishments employing 1000 workers or more used subcontractors. The average number of subcontractors per enterprise was 160 [18, *112*]. The system was most common in electrical goods, transportation equipment, textile mill products and machinery. It was least common in petroleum, food processing and ceramics. Characteristically, the parent company or companies provided a market for the semi-finished product and also supplied finance, raw materials, ma-chines (often secondhand), technical assistance, managerial advice and, sometimes, design specification and quality control. The economic viability of this system, as opposed to seemingly more rational intrafirm vertical integration, was a function of the social and factoral peculiarities of Japan. The advantages to the con-tractor were in market stability, labour costs and oligopolistic bargaining power. Part of the risk of demand fluctuations was passed on to dependent firms who usually bore the main brunt of recessions. In addition, utilising the traditional sector avoided rigidity in the labour market. In so far as large firms had a permanently employed workforce and a *nenkō-joretsu* (seniority payment) wage system, they were faced with fixed labour costs, even in a slump. The burden of unemployment and underemploy-ment was borne by dependent companies.

The main labour benefit was the typically lower wages available in dependent firms. Where large companies were in a monopolistic position they could dictate the prices of both finished products and supplies of materials and finance. The gulf in wages, conditions and techniques between a small sweat shop and a modern assembly plant was striking. However, many small firms had more than one customer. Some grew from small-scale to medium size and, less commonly, to large. Furthermore, the viability of the system was supported by other than pure economic rationality. As Hirschmeier and Yui [56, *339*] point out, it was based also 'on mutual trust and loyalties which play such vital roles in Japanese business'. In most countries small businesses decay because of their inability to compete with the large-scale sectors. In Japan many survived because they were complementary to it rather than in competition. They took advantage of their greatest assets, entrepreneurial flair and low labour costs. While the system involved inequality and social costs, in the light of Japanese factor endowments and inherited institutions, it made a positive contribution to manufacturing growth.

The major role in modern industrialisation was taken, not by small-medium enterprises, but by large enterprise groupings such as the *zaibatsu*. The 'old' *zaibatsu*, supported by the state and dominated by Mitsui, Mitsubishi, Sumitomo and Yasuda, reached their zenith at the end of the Second World War when they controlled one-quarter of the paid-in capital of incorporated business. They were dissolved by the occupation powers but reassembled in different forms. The co-existence of these giant oligopolies and small units in agriculture and manufacturing elicited the phrase 'dual structure', allegedly coined in the Japanese context by Hiromi Arisawa in 1957, although Boeke had pioneered the concept of social dualism as early as 1914. This dualism or, more aptly, differential structure [110] is central to many economic and political interpretations of Japan's experience. Models of unlimited supplies of labour and the labour surplus economy are based on the elastic supply of labour from the low wage 'traditional' to the 'modern' sector. The observed wide spectrum of techniques was partly a function of differential wages. Dualism provided the opportunity for exploiting with 'appropriate' technology the relatively abundant and cheap factor, labour. However, the widening gap in the 1920s and especially during the slump, between capitalists, landlords and the '*samurai*' of the labour force [89, *112*] on the one hand, and relatively impoverished tenants and small-scale industrial workers on the other, gave rise to social disorders and political upheavals. These in turn have been linked to the totalitarianism and imperialism of the 1930s [28, *115*].

3
The Tokugawa background
(c. 1600–1860)

The thesis of a dramatic, discontinuous transformation from feudal backwardness to twentieth-century industrialisation is no more tenable for Japan than that of an industrial *revolution* for Britain. The Tokugawa economy was producing a large surplus above peasant self-consumption, though much of it was 'wasted' in unproductive outlays. The potentiality for rapid growth existed but was constrained by the objects of the state and by its policy of seclusion. The Meiji Restoration was to reduce the remaining shackles on home and overseas markets and to permit greater freedom for individuals to respond to economic forces.

The Tokugawa era dates from the early seventeenth century. While the titular ruler of Japan remained the emperor in Kyoto, the effective rulers were the Tokugawa Shoguns at Edo (later Tokyo). The Shoguns owned about one-quarter of the agricultural land, the remainder being controlled by *daimyo* or lords in over 200 domains or fiefs. The *Bakuhan* system symbolised the relationships between the *bakufu* (central government) and the *han*, the domains of the quasi-independent lords. In principle, under the lords was a rigid fourfold Confucian-type hierarchy, *shi-nō-kō-sho*, of *samurai*, peasants, artisans and merchants, which in practice became more flexible. The *samurai*, numbering up to 2 millions in the nineteenth century, were feudal retainers, characterised as parasitic but from whose ranks were to spring some of the leaders of modern Japan. The farmers formed up to 80 per cent of the population and their rice taxes provided the main revenue. The artisans lived largely in the castle towns and satisfied the demand for luxury goods. As illustrated by the slogan *kikoku-senkin* (revere grain, despise money), the merchants were the lowest class, but they were growing in wealth and power, running the Shogun's finances and collaborating with the *daimyo* in the marketing of rice. The rulers could not control the merchants as they attempted to organise the peasants with regulations on land allotments, well-defined feudal levies and restrictions on crops and mobility. Instead, attempts were made to 'feudalise' the merchants by giving them official honours and status. Some actually became *samurai* and if they did not lead the eventual revolution, they oiled its wheels. Pre-1868 Japan is widely described as feudal and even as the classic case of feudalism, but uncritical acceptance of the feudal model encourages exaggerations about Tokugawa 'backwardness' and the revolutionary nature of the mid-nineteenth-century transition [47; 80].

Maintaining the hegemony of Shogun rule required a delicate balance between the centre and the fiefs to ensure the 'pax Tokugawa'. *Bushido,* a code of chivalry with emphasis on loyalty, and the structure and ideology of the *ie,* provided the social framework on which authority was based. *Ie* refers to a corporate, distinct resident social group, be it family, firm, establishment or company [102, 4; 179]. The Shoguns' power also depended on the vastly superior size of their estates, on a system of enfeoffing and abolishing *daimyo* lands and on *sankin-kotai,* or alternate residence. Under *sankin-kotai* the *daimyos'* families normally resided permanently in Edo as hostages to the Shogunate, while they and their retainers lived there in alternate years.

The third Tokugawa Shogun, Iemitsu, in the 1630s adopted the policy of *sakoku* or closing the country [55]. Japan had long been subjected to Chinese cultural, social and religious influences and borrowed and adapted Chinese technology; but even Kublai Khan in the thirteenth century could not achieve a military invasion, perhaps due less to Japanese naval prowess than to a *kamikaze* or divine wind. The sixteenth century saw the arrival of the Portuguese, the Jesuit Francis Xavier, the Roman Catholic religion and the smooth-bore musket, one of the earliest imports of western technology, rapidly diffused and produced by the gunsmiths of *daimyo* such as Oda Nobunaga. There followed other Europeans, especially the Dutch, the pilot of one of whose ships was Will Adams. Christianity and the Portuguese were increasingly regarded as undesirable foreign influences and Christianity as an organised religion ceased in 1638 with the massacre of 'rebel' Christians at Shimabara. There are echoes in the nationalistic expressions of the 'expel the barbarian' school in the mid-nineteenth century and in the reaction to communism in the 1930s.

In the 1630s Xenophobia was reinforced by edicts forbidding the construction of oceangoing vessels, prohibiting the overseas travel of Japanese and restricting foreign residents to a handful of Chinese and Dutch merchants. Isolationism did not prohibit some limited knowledge of western languages, science and technology in schools of Dutch studies [42]. Keene [70] has warned against overemphasis on the rigidity of *sakoku*. Kaempfer [68, *II, 174*] notes that at Nagasaki in the late seventeenth century the Dutch bought for export, 'boxes, camphor, tea, marmelade [sic], umbrellas and gold'. Japanese imports were mainly sugar, spices, looking glasses, textiles and raw silk and silk stuffs from China. Dutch military learning was copied in the Saga *han* to produce the first reverbatory iron furnace for guns in 1850, three years before Perry [153, *4*]. A significant handful of *samurai* realised long before the Restoration that although the Japanese might be superior in spiritual and cultural matters, the key to advance in industry and armaments lay in foreign technology.

However, apart from the few Chinese and Dutch contacts and the illegal overseas excursions of some *samurai*, *sakoku* essentially cut off Japan at a time when the West was making rapid economic development and the first industrial nation had 'taken-off'. Markets were limited to domestic demand, excluding export-led growth. In the Marxist view, isolationism constrained capital accumulation by bourgeois merchants and allowed 'feudalism' to persist beyond its 'natural' limits. The most damaging results were the virtual exclusion of post-Newtonian science and European economic and technological progress. 'A closed country meant a necessary condition of relative backwardness' [114, *6*]. On the other hand, Frank [36, *154*] argues that Japan avoided his 'development of under-development' syndrome because she escaped economic and political colonisation. *Sakoku* protected native manufactures, the decline of which in countries such as India was allegedly a factor in economic retardation. Morishima [89, *64*] even opines that 'the Bakufu had, quite unconsciously, implemented a perfect protective trade policy'. Further, the promotion of Japanese-style Confucianism, in so far as it was intellectual and rationalistic, bred mental attitudes ready to assimilate western science and technology and trained a large body of *samurai* in the bureaucratic and organising skills and the discipline which were invaluable for running the Meiji government and the modern army and factories. Searchers for legacies conducive to modern growth can find plenty of positive factors in autarchy.

The main concern in the current economic literature is about the state and development of the pre-1868 economy. While nobody now would subscribe to a view of uniform stagnation, far less to the 'sleeping warrior' theory that Perry's black ships suddenly awakened Japan to modern realities, there is a vigorous controversy about the emphasis to place on progress or back-wardness, particularly in respect of the later Tokugawa era. Part of the great Marxist debate of the 1920s was about the extent of pre-1868 'manufactories'. 'Pessimists' such as Norman [106, *20–5*] paint a picture of 'Asiatic wretchedness', usury, excessive taxation, famines, infanticide, 'poverty-stricken but proud retainers' and peasant rebellions – corrosives leading to the collapse of feudalism. The unpropitious 'Marxist view' is summarised and criticised by the arch revisionists Hanley and Yamamura [50].

A perusal of European travellers' writings dispels any notion of blanket backwardness. Kaempfer [68, *I*, 185; *III*, *7*] maintained that 'the Japanese are as good Husbandmen as perhaps any people in the world' and noted that 'nothing can be imported from abroad, but what some artist in this capital [Miaco/Kyoto] will undertake to imitate'. Golovnin [41, *32*] observed that the Japanese were 'much inclined to imitate all that is foreign'. If they had a ruler like Peter the Great 'with the resources and treasures which Japan possesses, he would enable it to become, in a few years, the sovereign of the eastern ocean'. Recent studies on demography, agriculture, commerce and living standards are clarifying a still obscure scenario.

Evidence on slow and regionally varied population growth is being accumulated by Hayami and the Keio school [52]. Expecta-tion of life was surprisingly high [50, *317*] and crude birth rates as low as 20 to 30 per thousand. While Mosk [92] finds low fecundity due to malnutrition, Smith [156, *147*], Nakamura [98; 99] and

Hanley and Yamamura [50, 9] point to conscious family planning 'to enjoy a rising standard of living'. At least for the late Tokugawa period the explanation of population control in terms of a Malthusian 'low level equilibrium trap' is giving way to one more consistent with growing per capita incomes and rising expectations.

Agriculture was the mainstay of the economy but the inadequacy of the data and regional, class and chronological variations produce conflicting views. To Broadbridge [14, *366*] 'urban Japan was a yawning mouth which sucked in the precious rice . . . which [the farmer] often could not afford to eat'. Rosovsky's [114, *4*] peasants were 'of a rather common Asian type . . . living on the border of subsistence'. On the other hand, Smith [154, *211*] describes the 'very high level of productivity in agriculture by the end of the Tokugawa period' and Umemura [111, *I*, *181*] 'a continuous process of growing agricultural production between late Tokugawa and Meiji'. Nakamura's 1966 study [97] caused 'rumbles in the rice fields' [136] by demonstrating the official understatement of agricultural production at the beginning of the Meiji period, largely due to land-tax evasion practices. This led not only to an exaggeration of Meiji output performance but also to an underestimation of late Tokugawa achievement. The key to agricultural advance was irrigation, improved seeds and the more widespread adoption on small plots of better methods of planting, weeding and applying insecticides and 'natural' and 'commercial' fertilisers. Meiji agrarian progress cannot be understood without reference to the backlog of indigenous biological techniques and water-control, gradually diffused among a receptive peasantry, usually highly organised in village communities, well-versed in communal infrastructure projects.

There were also advances in manufacturing and commerce [23]. Kaempfer [68, *III*, *6*] in the seventeenth century was impressed by the number of artificers and manufacturers in 'Osacca' and particularly by the scale of the 'sacki' brewing industry which not only sent products all over Japan but also exported them through Chinese merchants. Much of industry was organised as bye-employment in peasant households and in the 'domestic' system, but there were also examples in bleaching, salt, soy sauce, sake and oil-pressing of firms producing a large output requiring considerable overhead capital with complex division of labour. Both Hauser [51] in the Osaka and Kinai cotton trade, and Nakamura [98] document the diaspora of processes and techniques from urban to rural areas, motivated by relatively high urban labour and raw material costs and guild restriction. In the later Tokugawa period, the growing proportion of Japanese farmers working in non-agricultural operations, de-urbanisation, especially the decline of castle towns, and accompanying 'rural-centred pre-modern growth' resulted in a wide dispersion of industrial skills and attitudes. In the phrase of T. C. Smith [155, *158*] these were essential 'building-blocks' for later industrialisation. He further argues that the distinctive pattern of growth in rural rather than urban areas, along with isolation, peace and 'a nearly unchanging population' explain why textiles became the leading sector in modernisation and why Gerschenkron's model of relative back-wardness is inappropriate for Japan. However, the Keio school is showing that population was not 'unchanging', 'leading sectors' are no longer fashionable, textiles have played a prominent role in most modern industrialisation processes and the relevance of Gershenkron's model, even in the case of Tsarist Russia, is disputed. Nonetheless, the peculiar proto-industrialisation under the Shoguns was a prerequisite for post-1868 development. As Hauser says, 'the Togugawa period . . . provided a backlog of cottage industrial and organisational experience which could be translated into skills necessary for a modern industrial labour force and modern economic growth' [51, *188*].

Although there was a surprising absence of wheeled traffic, early European travellers noted the excellence of the main highways and the extent of internal commerce. Eighteenth-century Japan had some of the largest cities in the world with estimated peak popula-tions in Edo and Kyoto of half-a-million each and Osaka 400,000, implying an advanced network of trade and communications [159, *27*]. *Sankin-kotai* necessitated the marketing of *daimyo* agricultural products in Edo, encouraging the growth of coinage and later paper currency. Much has been written about the merchants [47; 56; 140; 177]. Mitsui in 1683 opened his Echigoya dry-goods shop where its successor, one of the largest department stores in Japan, still stands [132]. By the end of the seventeenth century it had hundreds of employees, paternalistic educational and welfare facilities, branch establishments and a form of double-entry book-keeping. Other urban and rural merchants and financiers made large profits at the expense of the rulers. However, unlike Weber's Protestants they did not imbue the 'spirit of capitalism' [56, 53], nor was 1868 a 'bourgeois revolution'.

Nakamura [98] stresses rural human capital accumulation in labour and managerial skills and entrepreneurial and innovative abilities, all 'helping to explain the exceptional growth performance of the Japanese economy in the last hundred years'. Dore [31; 65, 100] estimates that, at the time of the Restoration, 40 to 50 per cent of all Japanese boys and perhaps 15 per cent of girls were getting some formal schooling outside their homes, and singles out as important Tokugawa legacies, 'attitudes to popular education, training in abstract analysis, . . . the development of a respect for merit . . . and the strengthening of a collective ideology'. Hanley's [49] venture into the notoriously difficult 'standard of living' field contradicts pessimistic views of commoners' material well-being and maintains 'if I had to chose where to live in 1850, I would rather live in England if wealthy, and in Japan if working class'. In the absence of adequate statistics, arguments will continue about discontinuities, relative backwardness and living conditions. None the less, the Meiji inherited a society which, within certain constraints, had a highly developed agriculture, an extensive marketing system, a tradition of authoritarian intervention in the economy and, above all, a relatively well-educated people with attributes of discipline, loyalty, frugality and responsiveness to economic incentives. A potential for modern economic growth existed. The Meiji Restoration in 1868 brought the fundamental political and institutional changes which improved the environment for Japan's accelerated economic development.

The nature and causes of this Restoration have provided a fruitful field of historical controversy among Japanese and other historians. It is a truism that the events of 1867–8 were the culmination of interconnected internal political, social and economic upheavals against a background of growing western penetration, facilitated by the 'unequal' commercial treaties of the 1850s. Huber [60, 3] finds it 'a domestic affair, in which the Western challenge figured only as a convenient instrumentality'. Most historians place more emphasis on external factors, with Hayashi

[54, *375*] describing the 'crucial impact' of the *kurofune* (black ships) in 1853 and Beasley [7, *36*] opining that 'it was the consciousness of the external threat . . . that was to bring a national crisis'.

To describe the revolution as proletarian or peasant or bourgeois is, at best, a gross oversimplification and, at worst, misleading. Norman [106] finds peasant rebellions and 'the harvest of peasant revolt' but also the destruction of feudalism 'from above', led by lower *samurai* financed by merchants. Totman [164] plays down the significance of class and socio-economic change, and focuses on the activities and leadership of the *Bakufu* itself. Its collapse was a function of its inability to cope with what were essentially political problems at home and especially with the western threat. Smith and others have called it an 'aristocratic revolution', although it was a peculiar aristocracy whose post-revolutionary reforms made the *daimyo* forfeit their lands, introduced conscription and generally abolished old aristocratic privilege. Huber's [60, *224*] reformers were the 'service-intelligentsia', especially in the Choshu *han*, whose target was the antiquated feudal system of injustice, privilege and extravagance. These *samurai* were idealists, with an ideology supplied by intellectuals such as Yoshida Shoin, and aimed to elevate merit in place of preferment by birth and to bring institutional change to reduce wasteful outlays and direct resources into more productive channels. The murder by *samurai* of Ie Naosuke in 1860, a leading official and, in Beasley's view the one man capable of ensuring *Bakufu* survival, paved the way for further anti-government upheavals and eventually the coup d'état led by Choshu and Satsuma troops. In January 1868 the Tokugawa ruler was stripped of his powers and the administration was formally handed over to the Emperor Meiji. The new slogan became *fukoku kyohei*, enrich the country, strengthen the army.

4
The role of the state

From 1868 governments have played a prominent part in Japanese economic development. Since the Second World War the 'success story' of 'Japan Incorporated' is widely attributed to an optimal growth-oriented mixture of state-planning and private enterprise [66; 126, *755*]. For the pre-war period, some place great emphasis on the positive impact of the state and others find that Ashton's 'spontaneous forces of growth in society that arise from ordinary men and women' built the modern Japanese economy [78, *587*]. Many of the Meiji's nation-building activities were dictated by pragmatism and short-term expediency, to find employment for ex-*samurai*, to encourage import substitution, to counteract an emergency specie drain, and to build military railways. *Fukoku kyohei*, inspired by Xenophobic nationalism, dictated rapid indus-trialisation, with little priority for welfare. Over time the theme increasingly switches to imperialistic expansionism, partly, given the nature of the leaders, an 'inevitable' evolution and partly a reaction to specific political and economic events. Just as feudal-ism's demise was triggered by an external factor, so 'bourgeois-republicanism' or 'modern democracy' was imposed on Japan after the Second World War by foreign occupying powers, with America once again in the van.

The usefulness of state statistics is constrained by the unquantifi-able impact of outlays on education, extension services, shipping subsidies and armaments, and by complexities of categorisation. The share of government appears less in constant than in current prices because the prices of goods and services purchased by the state rose relatively to general prices. Tentative conclusions are that pre-Second World War the government was spending a higher proportion of GNP than after the war, that the state ratio was rising but fluctuated widely and that military outlays were significant. Since the Second World War total government expenditure as a percentage of GNP in Japan has been low compared with that in most developed countries with relatively small commitments for defence and welfare [126, *213*]. Pre-war, Nakamura's [101, *168*] ratio of 'all Government net spending' to GNE averaged 29 per cent 1910–14 and 50 per cent 1935–9. The respective shares of the private and public sector in gross domestic fixed capital formation excluding military investment were about 80 and 20 in 1887 and 1938 but in 1925 after the earthquake, 60 and 40 [116, *27*]. Purchases of goods and services accounted for some 80 per cent of pre-Second World War expenditure. Transfers to households were relatively small but there were subsidies to transport, especially shipping, in the nineteenth century and to ship-building and agriculture in the twentieth. Oshima [83, *370*] classified central and local government expenditures into four groups. Dominant are State Services (legislation, fiscal expenses, foreign affairs, justice and military) with 52 per cent in 1920. Economic Services (transport, agriculture and manufacturing) had a smaller but rising share with 23 per cent. Social Services (including education, health and welfare) were 12 per cent in 1920 and 'the rest' 13 per cent. The most controversial item of state expenditure and one of the most difficult to quantify, was 'military'. As a percentage of GNE military expenditures between 1885 and 1940 range from a little over 2 per cent in the early 1890s to 18 per cent in 1940 and a record 24 per cent in 1905.

In the early period the tax system was highly regressive, with progressive taxes assuming increasing significance in the twentieth century. As a percentage of central government tax receipts the land tax comprised about 74 per cent in 1870, declining to under 5 per cent in 1930 [128]. The share of excise taxes on sake, tobacco, sugar, soya, and textiles plus profits from some state monopolies increased from 10 per cent in 1880 to over 37 per cent in 1930. Income and business taxes formed under 2 per cent of central tax take in 1890, rising to 22 per cent in 1930. Customs duties varied from a low 4.5 per cent in 1880 to nearly 9 per cent in 1900. There were additional local taxes [39; 40; 111, *86*; 116, *199*].

The early Meiji governments widely indulged in deficit financing and apart from the 'Matsukata deflation' of the 1880s and restrictions in the 1920s there was a substantial rise in the ratio of the quantity of money to nominal GNE and very high statistical correlation between money supply and prices [101, *13*]. From 1887 to 1935 the personal consumption price index shows an annual average rate of growth of nearly 3.5 per cent [116, *220*]. Moderate rates of inflation combined with a suitable tax policy diverted resources from private consumption to the state and also to capitalists who, on the whole, had a high propensity to save and invest in growth-creating activities.

We find a secular increase and upsurges in borrowing in the 1870s related to the communication of ex-*samurai*'s stipends and pensions and to the Satsuma rebellion, in the 1890s and 1900s due to the wars with China and Russia, and in the 1920s connected with earthquake reconstruction outlays. However, the biggest wave of new debt issue was in the 1930s when borrowing accounted for one-half or more of total revenue.

The early Meiji government inherited some outstanding foreign debt and floated two loans in London in 1870 and 1873 for the first railway from Tokyo to Yokohama and to cover pension commutation [78, *179*]. They were redeemed in 1881 and 1897 and, apart from some short-term commercial credits, there was no more foreign borrowing until 1897. Only 6 per cent of the outstanding national debt was foreign in 1877 and 0 per cent in 1897. Japan was, therefore, unusual among developing countries in her small reliance on external capital in the initial stages of modern growth [93]. Matsukata [120, *I, 375*] maintained that 'neither the Government nor the people favoured foreign debts because, as the world's history shows, such obligations were liable to cause trouble politically between the two countries concerned'. Currency and exchange uncertainties before the adoption of the gold standard in 1897, unease about political stability and the absence of readily exploitable primary commodities coupled with restrictions on land-holdings by non-Japanese, did not present a favourable climate in the eyes of overseas capitalists. The cost of further borrowing and therefore the debt-servicing burden, was likely to have been much higher than, say, in India where guaranteed railway companies could raise funds at 5 per cent and less. Independence from foreign loans had positive advantages but it

placed a short-run burden on consumers, especially on the peasantry, and may have retarded early growth.

Victory over China in the war of 1894–5, the Chinese indemnity
of 360 million yen payable in sterling, the adoption of the gold
standard in 1897 and the Anglo-Japanese Alliance of 1902 which,
according to Beasley [7, *170*] put Japan 'on a footing of equality
with the greatest of the Powers', all dramatically altered the climate
for foreign rentiers. A loan could now be floated in London at only
4.4 per cent. The necessity to look abroad was a function of both
fast industrialisation and increasing military outlays culminating in
the expensive war with Russia in 1904–5. There were large deficits
on the balance of payments current account, peaking at 362
million yen in 1905, and amounting to over 1000 million yen from
1904 to 1913 [116, *334*]. The result was a large inflow of foreign
capital from 1897 to 1914. By 1914 about 60 per cent of the
national debt was foreign-held. The 'dependency syndrome' was
avoided because national and municipal governments did 85 per
cent of the borrowing, Japanese corporations 9.5 per cent, whereas
direct investment by foreigners was only 5.5 per cent. Reubens
[78, *227*] sees the developmental process as one of 'limited secular
disequilibrium', with a persistent tendency for demand to exceed
supply, a tendency evinced in moderate inflation and encouraging
investment and growth. The essential role of foreign capital was, at
critical periods, to prevent imbalances getting out of hand. The
First World War transformed the balance of payments and allowed
the accumulation of reserves which, along with some net capital
inflows, met foreign exchange requirements. By the 1930s Japan
herself was investing heavily overseas, particularly in the empire.

An evaluation of the role of the state involves more than an
analysis of revenue and expenditure. The early twin tasks of
government were to disband the remnants of feudalism and to
introduce a socio-economic and legal framework compatible with
development. The clan system was abolished and the ex-*daimyo*
sweetened, in some cases with new peerages and in all by the
commutation of their former revenues into state bonds. For some
ex-*samurai* there was commutation of stipends into less valuable
bonds, employment creation in administration and education,
loans for business including banking, and commissions in the
armed forces. Favoured capitalists, political merchants, were

allowed to buy up state enterprises cheaply, received contracts, subsidies and tax concessions and some became the powerful oligopolistic clique, the *zaibatsu*. Social relations in agriculture were the object of the Meiji land reform and land tax revision of the 1870s. A consolidated land tax was introduced in 1873, with later amendments, based at the fixed rate of 3 per cent of the assessed value of the land, payable annually in money and, unlike its predecessors, not fluctuating with the harvest [9]. The revision in tenure was less a revolution than the *de jure* recognition of the *de facto* existence of agrarian market relations and a landlord–tenant structure.

The main positive contributions of the Meiji government were institutional change and the creation of an infrastructure. In these, the eclectic nature of the foreign influence is striking. The criminal law was a mixture of Japanese feudal law and the *Code Napoléon*, while British and especially German models were taken for the commercial and civil laws. Prussia provided a pattern for municipal government. The universities resembled American and the schools, French. The French and Germans influenced the army and the British, the navy. Builders looked to London's Regent Street when reconstructing parts of Tokyo after the 1872 fire. The national banking system followed American lines and technology and personnel were imported from a variety of industrialised countries. Missions were sent abroad and there was limited support for Japanese studying overseas, especially in science and technology [16]. The attitude to foreign culture was suspicious and epitomised in the statement of Jo Niijima that 'one who wants to resist alien ideas and religion should thrust himself into its [*sic*] bosom and make its weapon his own' [58]. But the slogan *bunmei kaika* (civilisation and enlightenment) did not prevent the retention of the Japanese language, to some [161, *197*] a 'formidable barrier', restricting the 'education' of the workers and the growth of the labour movements, but to others a protection afforded against undue westernisation.

Foreigners were to be utilised and dispensed with as soon as possible, partly because they were costly. The principle *shokusan kogyo* (develop industry, promote enterprise) necessitated foreign advisers, managers and technicians including British, Dutch, French and German scientists, manufacturers and engineers such as Jardine's representative in tea, Glover in coal-mining, Verny in iron, Morrell and Trevithick in the College of Technology in 1877 and a total of 527 government-employed foreigners in peak year 1875. However, the Japanese take-over was rapid and the numbers fell to 155 in 1885. According to Jones [67] between 1868 and 1912 the government employed 3000 *yatoi* (hired menials) or *oyatoi gaikokujin* (honourable hired foreigners), half of them British, mainly in the first two decades. They were under strict financial and administrative control and were regarded as 'live machines', mere instruments and 'information brokers'.

The ability of Japan to substitute her own personnel for foreigners owed much to the promotion of education 'second only to national unity and defense in its pervasive significance for industrialisation' [82, *510*]. In vocational and technical training the private sector dominated, with on-the-job training and continuation schools designed to meet the specific requirements of large-scale industry. The Meiji established a Ministry of Education in 1871, gradually introduced compulsory primary education, set up secondary schools, technical colleges and universities [5], which were supplemented by private schools and colleges. By the turn of the century, more or less 100 per cent literacy was claimed. However, education also became a propaganda vehicle for emperor worship and nationalism, fostering 'ugly chauvinism' [145, *119*] and a combustible mixture of theocracy and industrial technology resulting in 'an irrational, uncalculating quest for the mystic aura of glory and grandeur – Japan's atavistic imperialism in Asia' [157, *228*].

Governments throughout were also directly and indirectly, through subsidies and controls, involved in many other aspects of the economy. Telegraphic and railway communications got high priority for strategic as well as economic reasons. The British were prominent in railways, with 'a Proposition for the Creation of a Source of Wealth for the Promotion of the Imperial Felicity and the Establishment of an Unlimited and Everlasting Benefit to the Nation'. Horatio Nelson Lay negotiated a loan in London, secured on Japanese customs revenue, and Morrell as chief engineer built the Tokyo–Yokohama line. Viscount Inouye [120, *435*], Superintendent of the Railway Bureau, has left an account of the political complexities, economic waste and extravagance of foreigners in the infant state-owned projects. He dispensed with overseas advisers and, in 1881, directed the completion of the Kyoto–Otsu line, the first built by Japanese. In the 1880s and 1890s, private enterprise took over but required substantial government support in the form of concessions and guaranteed rates of return. In the 1880s, 36 per cent of all state subsidies went on railways, a proportion only exceeded by that in ship-building. Nationalisation of major trunk lines was implemented in 1906 and private capitalists were bought out with generous compensation. Despite uneven progress, a comprehensive network was laid down with 7000 miles open in 1914 and over 14,000 in 1934 [3, *212*]. In addition Japan had acquired the South Manchuria Railway by her victory over Russia in 1906, an enterprise closely connected with the exploitation of the Chinese mainland [139].

Japan's rise to world dominance in ship-building and the merchant marine provides another example of state interest, in this case, apart from the navy, largely through the support and control of private enterprise [125, *129*]. In the 1870s and 1880s the state sold off most of its yards to big business. Mitsubishi, for example, acquired the Nagasaki yard for less than half of what the government had invested in it. State assistance took the form of directed subsidies both to ship-builders and the merchant marine, geared particularly to size and quality. Between 50 and 90 per cent of all state subsidies before 1914 went to this sector. By 1939 Japan launched over 13 per cent of the world's gross tonnage, second only to Britain. Thirty years later it was to lead with over 50 per cent [125, *130*].

Railways and shipping had military significance as did their ancillary, iron and steel. Despite the lack of iron ore and technological inexpertise, the government early determined to develop an iron and steel industry. The State Yawata Iron Works began production in 1901, but there were severe teething difficulties and the enterprise was not profitable until 1910. During and after the war there was a rapid increase in production both from the Yawata works and new private companies, which joined to form the semi-public Japan Steel Works in 1934. Apart from iron and steel, direct government ownership of manufacturing enterprises was rare from the 1880s. By 1912 only 12 per cent of 'factory' operatives were employed in government establishments.

Government influence on industrialisation tended, therefore, to be indirect through its fiscal, monetary and exchange rate policies, banking, protection, the encouragement of cooperation and rationalisation and promotion of exports. There were quasi-public banks such as the Yokohama Specie Bank, the Industrial Bank of Japan and the Hypothec Bank, often in collaboration with the big five *zaibatsu* banks and special institutions for colonial development such as the Banks of Taiwan and Chosen, which had a chequered and sometimes scandalous career. Yamamura [178, *243*] has warned against exaggerating bank participation in industrial financing, for example in the case of the Osaka Cotton Textile Company. However, the underdevelopment of a public market for securities meant that much of the corporate sector was subject to over-borrowing and indirect financing; savings, that is, were channelled to industry via the banking sector. The evolution of a sophisticated, modern system of financial institutions was a necessary condition for industrialisation. In the early stages, as Teranishi [113, *304*] points out, government credit, especially through the Bank of Japan, was crucial in the establishment of the private banking system. As in other fields, over time private individuals and enterprises responding to profit potentialities became as, if not more, important than the state.

Before the First World War the government encouraged importsubstitution but significant tariff protection did not exist, an experience dictated by the unequal treaties [82, *539*] and unusual among independent developing countries. The war provided its own protection but in the 1920s Japan adopted a policy of selective tariffs with heavy duties on luxury imports, on a wide range of manufactures, especially finished and consumer goods and, at the insistence of the farm lobby, controls and duties on foodstuffs. Aims were to support infant industries such as rayon, to restrain consumer imports and to exempt essential raw materials. In addition there was a vigorous policy through, for example, the *kokusan-shoreikai* (society to encourage domestic manufacture) of purchasing domestic products where this was viable. The remarkable expansion of exports was not mainly due to direct state intervention although the 1931 yen devaluation helped and there was encouragement of quality control, cooperation and rationalisation under the 1925 Exporters' Association Law and the Major

Export Industries Association Law [66, 98]. Industrial rationalisation (*sangyo gōrika*), with an emphasis on elimination of undue competition, scientific management, standardisation, economies of scale and support of domestic industries became a dominant theme in the Ministry of Commerce and Industry in the late 1920s and 1930s. Johnson [66, 115] calls this 'a period of indispensable gestation in the evolution and perfection of a genuine Japanese institutional invention, the industrial policy of the developmental state'.

There is a Gerschenkronian view that, because Japan lacked some basic prerequisites for growth at the time of the Restoration, the state had to fill the gap. Norman [106, 111] opines that merchant capitalists were reluctant to become industrialists, 'so the government . . . had itself to develop industry', and Smith [153, 36] that 'merchants almost to a man stuck resolutely to traditional fields of activity'. The positive contribution of government was to establish model factories, import foreign technology and technicians and, having made the initial break-through, to sell out to the private sector. However, Yamamura [175] has queried the lack of initiative of the *chonin* which allegedly left the entrepreneurial role to *samurai*-bureaucrats and *samurai* bankers and industrialists. There is agreement that 'situational imperatives' such as the employment of *samurai*, the need to counteract a specie drain, the absence of some essential raw materials, liaison with the *seisho* (political merchants) and pressing military needs, rather than conscious long-term planning, dictated much government activity. It is clear, also, that far from being exemplary models, many government enterprises experienced shortage of cash, technological blunder and managerial inefficiency. The Tomioka silk mill is widely quoted as a government-owned model of technological diffusion, but there is also evidence that outsiders were refused access to examine, far less to copy, the plant's machines and organisation [178, 226]. There were problems in the *chiku ho* coal mines and the state-owned Kamaishi iron-works were a technical failure. The cotton industry is one of Japan's success stories. Although it was peculiar in the instability of its labour force, there was a high degree of technological cooperation among firms and, through the agency of Platt Brothers of Oldham, the transmission and diffusion of best practice techniques. Unusually, this industry produced a pioneering innovation, the Toyoda automatic loom and, in 1929, allowed Platt's to manufacture it in England. Progress in the many small-scale mills in cotton was as Saxonhouse says, 'for the most part, fostered neither by the great *zaibatsu* nor by the Japanese Government' [125, *97*]. Indeed Koh [75, *35*] paints a picture of abject failure in early state cotton enterprises and states that the industry began to flourish only when it was 'liberated from the direct guidance of the government'. It is hardly surprising that attempts to initiate modern industry were marred by bureaucratic bumbling, technical errors and economic wastes and that, apart from some 'commanding heights' such as telegraphs, railways, iron and steel, and arsenals and dockyards, the government in the 1880s decided to dispose of its enterprises. The motives for this *volte-face* were due more to opportunism and the necessity of expenditure cuts than to an ideological switch from paternalism to *laissez-faire*. Tipton's [163] general view is that government policy hindered broadly based economic growth, led to war and destruction and, in particular, that direct industrial investment by the new Meiji state 'was neither extensive nor successful'.

Policy from the Meiji Restoration to 1945, except for a short period in the 1920s, was intimately bound up with defence, militarism and imperialism, culminating in a complex mixture of feverish political extremism in the 1930s [48, *133*; 59; 88, *228*]. This is not the place to attempt an explanation of the complex political, military, strategic, structural, social and economic factors behind Japan's wars and colonialism. There were particular reasons behind peculiar incidents at specific times and underlying threads which are related to more general theories of imperialism, especially of the Marxist–Leninist kind.

The need to exploit overseas empire markets because of 'minimal purchasing power at home' is a well-worn theme in the literature, particularly on the left. The interwar slump and, especially, the collapse in the American demand for silk, British Imperial Preference, and tariffs and other restrictions by the West on Japanese exports, encouraged a reactive imperialism and the development of Asian markets. In constant prices the rate of growth of exports in the period 1930–8 was over 8 per cent per annum. In the mid-1930s over 60 per cent of exports were going to Asia and nearly 40 per cent to Korea, Formosa and Manchuria.

Reduced dependence on foreign imports was at once a motive behind government promotion of domestic industry and for the exploitation of empire raw material supplies. In 1931–40, 58 per cent of the value of imports were primary products, of which crude foodstuffs comprised 18 per cent and raw materials 40 per cent. Nearly 30 per cent of Japanese imports came from the empire in the mid-1930s. But, in 1936, 'dependent' areas still supplied only 15 per cent of industrial material imports [82, *536*]. While economic imperialism was a factor in military adventurism, political and strategic elements were also important, and the net gains from empire are doubtful.

There is no consensus about the effects of military outlays on growth or the direction of causation. Investment in armaments is 'wasteful', but it may boost demand and, if supply is elastic, utilise idle resources and bring new resources into activity. For the Meiji period, Kelley and Williamson [71, *124*] find a deceleration in growth in 1895 to 1907 coinciding with high military outlays, and diminished military expenditures from 1907 to 1915 associated with a recovery in growth. If a peacetime strategy had been pursued, the rate of growth of GNP 'would have been raised by almost 0.5 percentage points'. Oshima's [83, *373*] thesis is that wartime deficit financing boosted purchasing power and economic growth followed, after the wars, by a fall in money incomes and a contraction of government demand leading to recession. There were low military expenditures and slow growth rate in the 1920s and high military expenditures and rapid growth in the 1930s. Ohkawa concludes that 'no long-term trends or swings can be related to the level of military spending' [116, *18*].

Whether or not defence needs crowded out private investment, they had an impact on the growth of some, especially heavy industries, and considerable technological spin-off. Ship-building and iron and steel were most closely connected with the state but defence needs also figured in the growth of the motor industry in the 1930s. Most cars in Japan had been assembled from imports of Ford and General Motors. The Automobile Manufacturing Industry law of 1936 licensed two Japanese companies, Toyota and Nissan, the state provided half of their capital, gave them tax and trade concessions and by 1939 the Americans were driven out of business [66, *132*]. Yamamura [176] powerfully argues the positive role of the 'strong army' policy and of the Chinese and Russian wars in technical progress, with illustrations from army and navy arsenals, shipyards and the Yawata ironworks. Moreover the private sector was aided not only by the technological spin-off from but also, at crucial junctures, by the demand induced by military investment. He concludes that Meiji militarism contributed positively to the establishment of some industries and to the country's technological base.

Militarism and imperialism brought positive gains. There were the Chinese indemnity, the benefits of joining the winning side in 1914–18, physical assets in the form of railways and mines, outlets for the employment of people and capital and the territorial acquisitions which Williamson and de Beuer [173] find more significant than Yamamura's technological spill-overs. On the other hand there were enormous costs and small returns, according to Boulding and Gleason [12, *257*], and Lockwood [82, *538*] thought it 'very likely that the whole program of empire building contributed little to the secular growth of the country's productive powers before 1938'. Japanese growth depended on a socio-institutional and political system with the capacity to respond to crises such as the western threat in the 1860s, the interwar slump and, more recently, the defeat and humiliation of the Second World War. While it is true that development depended on the actions of individual industrialists, peasants and factory workers responding to material incentives, they operated in an environment conditioned by a nation-state pursuing the goals of national greatness and, therefore, of a strong army and industrial growth. It may be impossible to quantify the role of the state and few would wish to emulate the course of Japanese history between 1868 and Pearl Harbour. But, in terms of its objectives, Japan was 'successful' before the Second World War. Modern economic growth and industrialisation owed much to direct and indirect government intervention, coercion and encouragement.

5

Factors in demand

Economic growth is a function of demand and supply factors interacting in a certain socio-institutional and political environment. Table 2 [116, *18*] provides the main categories of aggregate

Table 2 *Percentage composition of gross national expenditure in current prices*

		PC	GC[c]	I[m]	I[d]	X	M	X − M
1887[a]	(T)	79.6	7.3	2.3	11.1	7.2	−7.5	−0.3
1897	(P)	78.0	7.4	5.0	12.6	9.7	−12.7	−3.0
1904	(T)	75.0	12.4	4.9	10.0	14.0	−16.3	−2.3
1911	(T)	76.0	8.1	6.2	11.3	15.1	−16.7	−1.6
1919	(P)	70.0	6.2	5.6	14.5	21.2	−17.5	3.7
1930	(T)	73.0	11.1	10.4	5.7	18.2	−18.4	−0.2
1938[a]	(P)	61.7	11.6	12.6	14.8	21.4	−22.1	−0.7
1953[b]	(T)	65.9	11.2		21.9	3.3	−2.3	1.0
1969[b]	(P)	54.3	8.6		36.0	11.7	−10.5	1.0

A smoothed series of 7-year moving averages except where noted.

PC = personal consumption
GC = government consumption
I[m] = military investment
I[d] = investment (excluding military except as noted in some other tables)
X = exports
M = imports
[a] Five-year average
[b] Three-year average
[c] Military investment is not included in government consumption in the prewar period but is included for 1953 and 1969. However, it was sufficiently small to make the post-war series comparable.
[d] Inventory change has been deducted from post-war GNE and investment to make the figures comparable to the pre-war ones. Inventory change was 2.9 per cent of 1953 GNE (with inventory changes included) and 4.2 per cent in 1969.

demand. Government's role has already been noted and we start here with exports.

Japan was unusual in that Tokugawa isolationism virtually prohibited overseas trade; but, in 1934–6 prices, the rate of growth of exports from 1887 to 1938 averaged over 7 per cent per annum. The share of exports in GNE doubled from 7 to 14 per cent between 1887 to 1904 and peaked at over 21 per cent in 1919 and in 1938. The incremental export ratio, the ratio of the increase in exports to increases in GNP was 8 per cent 1876–80 to 1894–8, 29 per cent from 1895–9 to 1911–15 and 39 per cent from 1921–5 to 1934–8 [74, *177*]. Japanese exports grew faster than world exports, faster than other variables and, in the cotton industry, the export–output ratio rose from 1.5 per cent in 1890 to nearly 56 per cent in the 1930s. The structural shift in the composition of commodity exports is evident in Table 3 overleaf [116, *135*].

The prominence of primary products in the 1870s, such as tea, dried fish, copper, coal and sulphur, would be more striking were the category to include silk, here classified as a semi-manufacture. Raw silk was Japan's major foreign exchange earner before the First World War. This 'God-sent merchandise' benefited from European silk-disease, was suitable for small-scale, labour-intensive operations and did not compete for land with the main foodstuff, rice [112, *303*]. Silk gradually gave way to cotton and rayon and those in turn to heavy manufactures, chemicals, metals and machinery. By 1940 Japan exported heavy manufactures worth 2000 million yen compared with imports of 1800 million yen.

The three outstanding features of import composition were, first, increasing import dependence on primary commodities, especially raw materials. By 1971 Japanese imports as a percentage of domestic consumption were 100 per cent in lead, bauxite, wool and cotton, 99.7 per cent in crude petroleum, and 99.3 per cent in iron ore [126, *386*]. Second is the remarkable import-substitution in consumer manufactures, notably textiles, a function of consumption patterns and the growth of domestic manufactures, aided after the First World War by protection. Third, an industrialising country remained dependent on imported capital and intermediate goods, a 'supply-constraint' resulting in balance of payments deficits. In the period 1868 to 1940, Japan had a surplus on current account in only 27 years, mainly in the early 1890s,

Table 3 Exports and imports: percentage distribution of components in current price (1874–1970)

Period	Imports (%) Primary products Total	Crude foodstuff	Raw materials Fuels	Other	Manufactures Total	Textiles	Other light manufactures	Heavy manufactures	Exports (%) Primary products	Manufactures Total	Textiles	Other light manufactures	Heavy manufactures
1874–83	8.8	0.7	5.0	3.1	91.2	54.0	17.8	19.4	42.5	57.5	42.4	6.9	8.2
1877–86	10.3	0.8	6.1	3.4	89.7	49.6	18.7	21.4	39.5	60.5	43.0	7.8	9.7
1882–91	18.7	5.0	6.4	7.3	81.3	37.4	17.4	26.5	33.0	67.0	45.6	9.0	12.4
1887–96	28.3	7.1	5.0	16.1	71.8	28.2	14.6	29.0	26.3	73.7	48.9	11.3	13.5
1892–1901	36.4	9.9	4.5	22.1	63.6	16.8	14.2	32.6	21.0	79.0	52.6	13.2	13.2
1897–1906	43.2	13.8	4.7	24.6	56.9	11.8	12.3	32.8	16.6	83.4	53.6	15.9	13.9
1902–11	45.2	12.5	4.0	28.8	54.8	9.6	10.8	34.4	14.1	85.9	53.8	17.2	14.9
1907–16	50.0	10.3	2.7	37.0	50.0	5.0	9.9	34.4	12.3	87.7	53.6	16.7	17.4
1912–21	52.6	12.5	2.2	37.9	47.4	5.5	8.5	35.6	9.0	91.0	56.4	15.3	19.3
1917–26	54.3	16.1	2.9	35.3	45.7	3.3	9.9	30.8	7.3	92.7	63.6	14.0	15.1
1922–31	56.6	18.8	4.3	33.5	43.4	5.7	11.6	26.3	6.8	93.2	65.8	14.5	12.9
1927–36	61.0	19.0	5.9	36.1	39.0	3.3	10.5	25.2	6.7	93.3	56.8	16.8	19.7
1931–40	58.0	17.5	7.6	33.0	42.0	2.4	8.3	31.3	6.9	93.1	45.7	18.7	28.7
1951–55	87.8	26.9	11.3	49.6	12.2	0.6	1.2	10.4	3.6	96.4	38.6	17.4	40.4
1956–60	77.3	14.8	16.5	46.0	22.7	0.5	2.0	20.2	4.2	95.8	31.6	19.9	44.3
1960–65	77.6	14.9	18.4	40.3	26.4	0.5	3.9	22.0	3.3	96.7	21.1	19.0	56.6
1966–70	70.8	14.4	20.6	35.8	29.2	1.3	4.5	23.4	2.4	97.6	14.4	12.2	68.2

Notes: All figures are percentage shares of total exports or imports calculated from ten-year (pre-war) or five-year (post-war) averages of current price series.

during the First World War and in most of the 1930s [116, *332*].
The deficits were met by short- and long-term capital inflows and,
in the 1920s, by a fall in overseas specie holdings.

Governments had and still have a prominent role in trade. In the
nineteenth century, while the depreciation of silver helped exports,
financial and currency stabilisation were important prerequisites
for international dealings, met by the foundation of institutions
such as the Bank of Japan and the Yokohama Specie Bank. The
Chinese indemnity of 360 million yen (£32.9 million) facilitated
the adoption in 1897 of that symbol of world status, the gold
standard. Dropped in the First World War, it was briefly restored
in 1930–1 as the culmination of the 'tight money' policies of the
1920s. In 1932 the devaluation of the yen is associated with an
explosion of exports, but a marked deterioration in the terms of
trade partly offset the growth in export volumes. Apart from
shipping and ship-building, subsidies were few although a limited
and selective policy of tax immunity and rebates was applied to
certain export industries such as textile fabrics. In the interwar
period there were attempts at 'rationalisation' through the Exporters Association Law and the Major Export Industries Association
Law, and by the 1930s the export guilds had virtually become
instruments of trade policy. 'Liberal' pre-war trade policy was
succeeded by protectionism and eventually by the development of
a yen bloc and 'co-prosperity sphere' in Asia [95]. Trade increasingly became dominated by what Yamamura [125, *161*] called the
'uniquely Japanese institution', the General Trading Company. Its
major role was in reducing risks arising from fluctuations in
demand and exchange rates, in promoting cost-reducing economies of scale in information services, transportation, linguistic and
technological learning-by-doing and in economising scarce capital
through its financial functions. In 1972 the ten largest trading
companies accounted for 51 per cent of total export values and 75
per cent of imports and they now are prominent multinationals.

There is much debate about export-led growth, about whether
exports were the handmaiden or the engine of growth, the result of
internal domestic supply and price conditions or of exogenous
overseas demand shifts. Rostow [138, *422*], for example, maintained that exports were a 'leading sector' and that 'Japan shares
with Britain the experience of a take-off based squarely on the

production and export of textiles'. On the other hand, just as the consensus on industrial revolution Britain is now that 'trade was the child of industry', so Ohkawa and Rosovsky [114, *173*] express the predominant view on Japan that 'the rate of growth of exports has been high . . . because the rate of growth of the economy has been high . . . and not vice-versa'. In fact there was a two-way causal interrelation between exports and growth – and the direction of causation varied for different commodities at different periods. Raw silk was an indigenous staple the exports of which were sensitive to overseas demand shifts. Over time, and particularly since the Second World War, internal supply factors increasingly conditioned the ability to export.

One measure of the relative significance of external demand compared with internal supply is the Caves' test [17, *425*; 11, *150*]. Export-led growth due to overseas demand would be reflected in a rise in both export prices and volumes. This syndrome is only apparent in the exceptional conditions of the First World War. From 1870 to 1970 there was a trend fall in the ratio of export prices to domestic prices and, from 1920, of Japanese export prices to world trade prices [116, *331*]. In most periods the main determinant of export growth was low, competitive prices [21, *220*]. These low prices were a function of many interacting internal supply conditions such as 'cheap labour', which elicited western accusations, especially in the 1930s, of 'social dumping'. Marxists suggested a vicious circle of low wages, due to a high rate of exploitation and capital accumulation, resulting in a constrained domestic market which in turn led to a drive for overseas markets, necessitating cheap labour. More significant was the lag between wages and productivity. Particularly after the First World War, when there was a rise in the share in exports of 'modern' manufactures compared with 'traditional' products such as raw silk, cost-reducing, productivity-boosting technological progress and economies of scale became decisive factors. According to Akamatsu's [2] 'Flying Wild Geese Pattern' exports were a function, not of restricted but of expanding domestic demand. His stages are a rise in internal demand, say for automobiles, import of cars, the establishment of import-competing domestic industries, increased output and lower costs, import-substitution and, in the final stage, exports. Yamazawa [113, *386*] describes the process of import growth, import substitution and expansion of exports as a 'catching-up product cycle'. Import-led rather than export-led growth is the description of choice in this scenario.

An interpretation in terms of internal supply and price effects does not exclude the view that exports were an important stimulus to development. The annual average rate of growth of exports from 1887 to 1938 (7 per cent) was more than double that of GNE (3 per cent), and faster than any of its components [116, *20*]. The share of exports in the final demand for manufactured products rose to a peak 30 per cent in 1930 [74, *89*]. Exports of manufactures were both the result of and, through backward-linkages, the cause of technical progress and, by widening the market, encouraged further scale economies. However, the vital role of exports was to provide foreign exchange for imports. It was the ability to exploit overseas markets for silk, tea and marine products which financed early industrialisation. Manufacturing both for home and foreign markets depended on imports of raw materials and inter-mediate and capital goods. Japan's development has been de-scribed as a process of closing the 'technological-gap' with the West. This required imports and, therefore, exports.

Table 2 shows consumption's share of GNE. Personal consump-tion comprised, in current prices, about 80 per cent in the 1880s, 62 per cent in 1938 and 54 per cent in 1969. The declining share is notable. In constant prices the trend rate of growth averaged 2.55 per cent per annum from 1887 to 1938 and 3.25 per cent per annum from 1887 to 1969. Per capita rates were 1.3 per cent and 2 per cent. Changes in consumer expenditures were a function of many interacting variables including the persistence of traditional tastes, the surprisingly small demonstration effect of western con-sumer imports at least until after the American occupation, a generally regressive tax system, moderate secular inflation, a high propensity to save even at relatively low income levels, a population growth rate of 1.2 per cent per annum and changes in the level rate of growth and distribution of income.

Very broadly Japanese average per capita disposable incomes throughout the modern period were much higher than in most LDCs such as India but, until very recently, much lower than those in developed western countries. The rate of growth of per capita incomes in constant prices was over 1.9 per cent per annum from 1887 to 1938 and 2.7 per cent per annum from 1887 to 1969. Evidence on its distribution is uncertain due to regional price variations, non-pecuniary benefits, especially significant in Japanese 'paternalistic' companies, and a large self-employed category whose income is derived from a mix of labour and capital. In recent years the enormous rise in the price of urban land has transferred wealth to some real asset holders, but data on capital gains are even less adequate than those on income. However, Japanese income since the Second World War has been more evenly divided than in most non-socialist developing countries and an estimate for 1965 of the Gini coefficient of 14 developed countries showed that Japan had a more equal personal income distribution than in all except Czechoslovakia and Hungary [11, *166*]. For the pre-war period there is no hard evidence. Per capita incomes were invariably lower for farm than for urban employee households, the intersectoral differential remaining stable down to 1915, increasing in the interwar period and narrowing markedly from about 1960 [125, *363*]. These rural-urban changes reflect changes in the economy as a whole [87]. From the Meiji Restoration to the present there was a slight trend to more even personal income distributions masking years of increased skewness in the 1920s and 1930s. Functional or factoral data give labour's relative share in the non-primary sector as 68.6 per cent in 1900, 67.2 per cent in 1925 and 58.3 per cent in 1938–40 [125, *371*; 116, *205*]. The empirical evidence is too sketchy to confirm Kuznets' postulate that modern economic growth tends to be accompanied by a widening, stabilising and then narrowing process of income distribution. Neither can one measure the extent of disadvantaged groups nor the social deprivation accompanying industrialisation which provokes growing concern about a welfare gap (*fukushi gappu*).

In absolute terms the majority of Japanese gained from a secular rise in living standards and real wages. Real wages declined in the 1930s but over the long run we find a moderate positive rate of growth from 1880 to 1939 of 0.34 per cent per annum in agriculture and 2.62 per cent in mining and manufacturing [116, *230*]. Further, between 1875 and 1970 the number of 'gainful workers' increased by 250 per cent with an accelerating annual average growth rate even in the 1920s and 1930s [116, *244*].

Underemployment existed in the traditional sector, but the amount of overt or formal unemployment was and still is negligible compared with that in developed capitalist societies. Patrick and Rosovsky maintain that 'it has never been a serious or even a minor problem' [126, *24*].

Consumption expenditure was dominated by food. In both current and constant prices its share was around 65 per cent in 1874–83, 60 per cent in 1912–21, but then fell markedly to 50 per cent in 1931–40 and about 35 per cent in 1962–71 [116, *160*]. While there was a marked absolute increase in expenditure on 'western' or 'superior' foods, notably since the Second World War, the Japanese diet remained weighted towards traditional products such as fish and, especially, towards rice which before the Second World War provided 60 per cent of the total calorific intake [53, *143*].

By 1979 Japan was now near the top of the table for consumer durables. Household ownership rates for refrigerators were 99 per cent, for colour televisions 98 per cent, nearly double the UK rate, and for washing machines 98 per cent [131, *135*]. But before the war, consumers were noted for 'innate conservatism', and Nurkse [107, *75*] opined that the Japanese imitated the West in all but consumption patterns. As late as 1955 about one-half of total consumer expenditures was on 'traditional' commodities [114, *159*]. Income elasticity of demand appears surprisingly low for all consumables and for food in particular [71, *152*; 112, *398*; 116, *169*]. Explanations in terms of relatively low incomes are not sufficient and sociologists point to the persistence of 'Oriental consumption habits' and the combination of 'Japanese ethos and Western technology'. While absolute increases in consumption were a major demand factor in growth, the declining share of personal consumer expenditure released resources for capital formation.

The fourth component of aggregate demand is investment. Capital formation poses serious problems of definition and data but investment in Japan has been allocated a crucial role especially since the Second World War. In real terms, gross investment jumped from 20 per cent of GNP in the early 1950s, to 40 per cent in the mid-1960s by which date the share of business plant and equipment investment alone was 20 per cent of GNP. The Soviets in the 1930s perhaps performed similarly but Patrick and Rosovsky [126, *18*] expressed a widely held view of Japan when they alluded to 'the most impressive investment performance ever achieved in any peacetime, democratic, market economy'. A key to the economic miracle is therefore to be found in the ability of entrepreneurs or rather corporations to respond to the profit opportunities arising from growth and technical progress and in the willingness of Japanese to devote so high a proportion of their resources to thrift that personal savings accounted for about one-third of gross savings.

There are no adequate statistics for the 20 years or so after the Restoration but from the 1880s there is a plethora of data. Table 2 demonstrates that the share of non-military investment in GNE was relatively stable until the First World War and, apart from the slump, increased modestly in the interwar period. The dramatic rise in investment was in the military component, a notable contrast with the post-Second World War period. The average annual rate of growth of total investment was 5.44 per cent from 1887 to 1938, slower than exports (7.02) but much faster than GNE (3.13) and personal consumption (2.55). There was a close relation between fluctuations in investment and the growth pattern of demand, leading Ohkawa and Rosovsky [114, *147*] to the conclusion that 'in Japan investment was the driving force of growth'.

6
Land and agriculture

Many economic historians find the main explanation of Japanese expansion in the supply side of the economy. In the remaining sections we consider the factors of production, land, labour, capital, technology and enterprise.

Japan demonstrates that a poor resource base and scarce cultivable land are not insuperable obstacles to development. She was deficient in industrial raw materials, particularly iron ore. The percentage of raw materials in imports had to rise from 8 in 1874–83, to over 40 in the 1930s and to a peak of 63 per cent in the late 1950s. Some 65 per cent of Japan is under forests. These were an important source of employment and income for peasants; raw silk depended on mulberry trees and timber was used in a variety of modern and traditional industries, including building, furniture and paper. Marine products provide up to half of the animal protein in the Japanese diet, and were significant in exports and a valuable source of fertilisers.

Agriculture's share of net domestic product in current prices fell from over 42 per cent in the late 1880s to 18 per cent in the late 1930s and to around 8 per cent in 1970 [116, 35]. The ratio of primary to total labour force fell from 75 per cent in 1880 to 43 per cent in 1940 and 20 per cent in 1970 [53, 6]. Output data have been the subject of frequent revisions, notably by Nakamura [97]. Uncertainty remains, especially about the nineteenth-century figures. While Nakamura's revised data were a useful corrective to earlier exaggerations, his own figures underestimated Meiji and overestimated interwar growth rates. Yamada and Hayami discuss the various estimates and their evidence is in Table 4 overleaf [116, 89].

Table 4 *Agriculture: output, input, and productivity growth rates and contributions to output growth in 1934–6 prices (in per cent)*

| | Annual compound rates of growth | | | Relative contributions to output growth by inputs and productivity | |
	Total output	Total input	Total productivity	Input	Productivity
1880–1900	1.6	0.4	1.2	25	75
(1880–95)	(1.4)	(0.3)	(1.1)	(21)	(79)
1900–20	2.0	0.5	1.5	25	75
(1905–20)	(2.0)	(0.5)	(1.5)	(25)	(75)
1920–35	0.9	0.5	0.4	56	44
1935–45	−1.9	−0.9	−1.0	47	53
1945–55	3.2	3.4	−0.2	106	−6
1955–65	3.6	1.0	2.6	28	72

Notes: Annual compound growth rates between five-year averages of the data centred on the years shown.

Japanese growth rates are much higher than in the UK in the eighteenth and nineteenth centuries, but lower than in post-independence India and some other LDCs. The spurt of growth at the beginning of the century coincided with a jump in the rice area planted with improved varieties from 4 per cent in 1895 to 30 per cent in 1905, a dramatic example of diffusion. The deceleration in interwar growth is notable as is the remarkable recovery post-Second World War due, *inter alia*, to land reform, a decline in the labour force, new technologies and state aid. In the Meiji period and post-Second World War, productivity increases contributed most to the rate of growth of output.

Agrarian achievement was a function of the Tokugawa legacy, of the application of inputs, of productivity boosting changes in technology and land infrastructure, of the incentives and disincentives available to cultivators and their 'rational' response to them. It also stemmed from government policies which, while generally squeezing resources from farmers, nonetheless allowed a 'suitable' socio-institutional environment and invested in the critical areas of education, research, extension services and transport. The Meiji did not inherit a uniformly backward agriculture. The Professor of Botany at Uppsala described the excellence of cultivation in the eighteenth century, especially the weeding, fertilising and transplanting of rice. Interdependent innovations included commercial fertilisers, seed selection and planting and the wooden *semba koki* for separating grain from stalk in rice [154]. Most important was an advanced irrigation system, the distribution of the water being determined, not by individual farmers, but through the cooperative agreement of *suiri kumiai* or water use associations [35, *34*]. Much of early Meiji technical progress was simply due to the diffusion of traditional technology by veteran farmers (*rōnō*).

Agricultural development since 1868 has taken place against an increasing 'land-resource constraint' with attempts to improve land-productivity through a seed-fertiliser technology, dependent on adequate irrigation. The mechanism and timing of these changes and their response to movements in relative factor costs are complex [63; 113, *67*] and revisionist views to the land-saving, labour-saving paradigm have been expressed by Nghiep [103], Grabowski and Sivan [45] and Grabowski [44]. Some light on the process is shed by an examination of the growth rate of inputs, noted in Table 5 overleaf [116, *88*].

While aggregate data conceal aspects of labour supply and quality, such as the 40 per cent increase in workdays per worker between 1880 and 1920, and there was a slight decline in labour inputs, most remarkable is the relative stability of the labour force and the persistence of a large 'reserve army' in farming. Closer scrutiny of the land input would reveal that much of the new acreage was in marginal and upland fields, particularly in Hokkaido, and that there was some switch from wet to dry rice cultivation and an increase in double-cropping. Rice was the main crop, contributing over half of total agricultural production as late as 1940. The pattern of rice output and yields per hectare was of accelerating growth until about 1920 followed by relative stagnation in the interwar period. Land continued to be farmed in small-scale family units. In 1940 less than 1.5 per cent of farms were larger than 5 hectares, over 57 per cent were between 0.5 and 2 hectares and over 33 per cent were less than 0.5 hectares. There was no substantial change in this distribution between 1900 and 1940. The growth of agricultural output was due, therefore, neither to a substantial rise in area cultivated nor to increases in the

Table 5 *Agriculture: annual growth rates of inputs (in percent)*

Period	Labour				Land			Fixed capital		Current inputs	
	Total input	Male	Female	Total	Paddy field	Upland field	Total	Machinery and implements	Total	Fertiliser	Total
1880–1900	0.4	0.1	0.1	0.1	0.2	0.8	0.5	0.7	0.9	1.6	1.8
1900–20	0.5	−0.5	−0.7	−0.6	0.4	1.1	0.7	2.0	1.3	7.7	4.7
1920–35	0.5	−0.1	−0.1	−0.1	0.3	−0.1	0.1	1.8	0.9	3.4	3.2
1935–45	−0.9	−1.7	2.0	0.1	−0.3	−0.6	−0.4	−0.2	−1.4	−4.9	−6.6
1945–55	3.4	1.5	0.3	0.9	0.3	0.1	0.2	3.0	2.0	13.4	15.0
1955–65	1.0	−3.5	−2.5	−3.0	0.3	−0.2	0.1	11.5	7.8	3.7	8.5
Pre-war period:											
1800–1935	0.4	−0.2	−0.2	−0.2	0.3	0.7	0.5	1.5	1.0	4.3	3.2
Post-war period:											
1945–65	2.3	−1.0	−1.1	−1.1	0.3	−0.1	0.1	7.2	4.9	8.4	11.7
Whole period:											
1880–1965	0.7	−0.6	−0.2	−0.4	0.2	0.3	0.3	2.6	1.6	4.1	3.9

Notes: Compound growth rates between five-year averages of the data centred on the years shown.

average size of cultivators' holdings, but rather to increases in land productivity.

Fixed capital grew faster, especially after the Second World War, than labour or land. However, there was no mechanical revolution until the relative rise in the price of farm labour in the 1960s. There were only 1000 power tillers in 1937 and no tractorisation [112, *155*]. Investment in buildings, irrigation and livestock rose but even by the late 1930s livestock's share of the value of total agricultural production was under 6 per cent. The share of 'capital interest' in total agricultural costs at 10 to 11 per cent in the 1930s remained far below that of labour wages and land rent and marginally below that of current inputs. Before 1940 Japanese agriculture was not capital-intensive.

By far the fastest rate of growth was of current inputs, pre-eminently of fertilisers. Investment in fertilisers, which had become mainly 'artificial' by the interwar period, was facilitated by their relatively low cost, by the 1899 Fertiliser Control Law which licensed the manufacture and controlled quality, and by the copying of German scientific methods. Technical progress was biochemical rather than mechanical and compatible with small plots and relatively small investments. The annual rate of growth of output per worker rose from 1.5 per cent 1880–1900 to 2.6 per cent 1900–20 and then decelerated to 1 per cent from 1920 to 1935. Output per hectare in the same periods was 1.1, 1.3 and 0.8 [116, *92*]. The interwar deceleration suggests diminishing returns to Meiji technology and caused government concern about future food supplies and the promotion of irrigation and drainage schemes. It was not until after the Second World War that new scientific techniques and mechanical changes were to boost output per worker during 1955–65 to 6.6 per cent per annum and, per hectare, to 3.5 per cent per annum. Techniques were often location-specific in that a rice strain suitable for Kyushu would be frostbitten in Hokkaido, and there was a complementary package of high-yielding varieties, fertilisers and adequate methods of planting, transplanting, ploughing and weeding. Most crucial were irrigation and drainage. The growing significance of off-farm purchases was illustrated by Ohkawa [112, *14*] when he divided current inputs into those of agricultural and non-agricultural origin and showed a much faster rate of increase in the latter. The

Meiji Nōhō (agricultural methods) could no longer be ascribed to the utilisation of agriculture's own resources, but to 'a two-way interdependence of agricultural-industrial development' [71, *170*] exemplifying the concurrent growth model.

Assuming that most peasants were neither 'inert' nor merely 'satisficing', improvement depended on incentives and 'rational' responses. Meiji government measures reduced transaction costs and market imperfections by abolishing feudal restrictions on commerce, crop selection and labour mobility and by developing a modern road and railway system. The ending of *sakoku* opened an overseas market for primary products, especially raw silk, and population growth, urbanisation and industrialisation provided a burgeoning demand for food and some raw materials. Market relations were fostered by the monetarisation following the change in tax payments [9] in 1873 from kind to money and peasants became aware of new 'incentive' consumables in trade centres. The annual growth rate of prices of agricultural products from 1887 to 1935 at 3.23 per cent was much faster than that for investment goods at 2.34 and manufactured goods at 2.17 [116, *220*]. Except during the Matsukata deflation from 1881 to 1885 and in the 1920s, farmers were faced with prices for their products which grew faster than other prices and changes in the relative prices of inputs and factors. Fertiliser prices fell by over 3 per cent per annum from 1890 to 1920 and all current input prices by over 2.5 per cent per annum. The relative scarcity of land was reflected in a rapid increase in its price pre-Second World War. Wage rates rose much more slowly until the 1960s. The relative changes in the price of factors dictated in rational producers a choice of land-saving technique using purchased inputs, especially of fertilisers.

Agricultural development depends not only on the availability of inputs and price incentives but also on the distribution of gains among classes and on the land tenure system. In Japan agricultural labourers were an unusually small class with numbers falling from 400,000 in 1920 to only 165,000 in 1941. Cultivation was typically undertaken by family farm households, the number of which remained fairly constant at about 5.5 millions, under a complex variety of part-ownership, full ownership and tenancy. Until the First World War there was some switch from owner-cultivation to tenancy. The percentage of cultivated land under tenancy rose from 37 per cent in 1883 to 46 per cent in 1914 [128], partly because the temporary collapse in rice prices during the Matsukata deflation made it difficult for some peasants to meet their cash tax obligations. Tenants gained least from agrarian progress and consumption per household of tenant farmers from 1890 to 1920 was only about 55 per cent of that of owner-farmers [125, *370*]. They had to dispose of their product after the harvest when prices were lowest and about half of their output was siphoned-off by landlords in rent in kind (rice). Even so many tenants gained from 'widening lags between increasing production and rents' which, according to Ranis [128], 'strengthened incentives among tenant tillers'.

Until the 1920s, when all agrarian classes suffered, incentives were much greater for owner-cultivators and, especially, for land-lords. A combination of a trend rise in rice and land prices, the profits from selling the produce of rents in kind and a land tax which was fixed and not related to output changes, meant growing real rewards for increased production and productivity. While there was a wide variety of individual wealth and attitudes among Japanese landlords, the current view is that what had been a paternalistic, innovating, cultivator class in the nineteenth century was increasingly characterised in the twentieth by absenteeism, parasitism and extra-agrarian pursuits [171]. Meiji landlords are described as 'energetic and keen agriculturalists' [28, *47*], 'a sharp contrast to Ricardo's wastrel type' [128], cultivating their own lands (*Tezukuri-Jinushi*) and typified by the 'paternalistic-progressive' Homma family [28, *44*]. They had the means and the knowledge to pioneer technological improvements. These were disseminated through Agricultural Discussion Societies (*Nōkai*) and Seed-exchange Societies (*Hinshukokankai*) and were more readily adopted because they were both relatively cheap and had been tried and tested to suit local conditions [64, *165*]. There was some identity of interest between landlords and tenants, with mutual recognition of duties and obligations, loans and rent reductions in bad years, community development of irrigation, rice inspection to improve quality and land adjustment schemes for the consolidation of scattered, fragmented holdings. It was of material advantage for landlords to promote improved methods which required village cooperation. An increased output of better quality rice enabled higher rents in kind or, at least, less necessity for costly rent reductions.

In the twentieth century and particularly after the First World War, the increasing commercialisation of agriculture, the growth in imports of colonial rice and the price falls of the 1920s saw changes. There was a growth of parasitic landlords and absenteeism, with renting rather than cultivation their main priority, and a rise in tenant disputes. There were also increasing non-agrarian outlets for landlords' investment and greater risks in cultivating rice. Agriculture in the 1920s and early 1930s became 'the sick man of the Japanese economy' [114, *98*] and output decelerated to 0.9 per cent per annum from 1920 to 1935.

At least until the 1920s, the government extracted more from the rural sector than it invested in it but, without large capital outlays, it contributed to growth through institutional and educational developments. In addition to fostering market relations through the Meiji reforms and outlays on transport, the state established Experiment Stations and Agricultural Colleges. The early strategy of imitating Europe and America and importing best-practice methods and machines changed to one of spreading indigenous techniques and promoting irrigation and methods which were both suitable for Japanese conditions and not too expensive [53, *50*]. Associations and societies such as the Agricultural Society of Japan (*Dai Nippon Nōkai*) were founded and laws such as the Arable Land Replotment Laws (1899) were passed to enforce land-improvement projects and consolidation of holdings. Access to credit on reasonable terms was tackled by Credit Cooperative Associations, the Hypothec Bank in 1897 and other Agricultural Banks which advanced low-interest loans for land improvements. There were also plenty of private money lenders but in the field of long-term agricultural credit the government's role was dominant. The Race Riots of 1918, imports from Korea and Taiwan, the decline and instability of prices in the 1920s plus growing landlord and tenant agitation occasioned Rice Laws to control rice prices through an Ever-Normal Granary Plan, a more vigorous promotion of self-help associations and cooperatives and greater state outlays on rural infrastructure. Attempts to satisfy tenant demands in the 1930s and to anticipate the later McArthur land reform by transforming tenants into owner-cultivators had very limited success in the face of opposition from landlords.

The contribution of agriculture to economic growth is difficult to assess. In the early stages of modernisation agriculture had a crucial contributory if not active leading role in the growth process. On the one hand it provided a market for industrial products and, on the other, it supplied resources of food, exports, labour and capital. Evidence is adequate on none of these, least of all on the market. The agrarian demand for the output of industry depends, *inter alia*, on the size and growth of the farm population, on incomes and on propensities to consume and save. The absolute number of gainful workers in agriculture fell little between 1872 and 1940 from about 15.5 to 14 millions [116, *392*] but the substantial decline in the proportion of farmers implies a relative contraction in the number of rural consumers. There was a trend rise in real disposable agricultural incomes but a gap between rural and urban real income and farmers' marginal propensity to save was much higher than that of non-agricultural wage and salary earners. There was no market for sophisticated agricultural machinery but 5 million farm households did generate considerable demand for off-farm inputs such as nails, implements and chemical fertilisers. The mere size of the Japanese rural sector indicates its significance but, over time, one must look increasingly to the non-agrarian domestic sector and exports for the main demand generators.

On the supply side of agriculture's 'role', there is also much speculation [46]. Although the share of 'crude' foodstuffs in imports rose from under 1 per cent in the 1870s and 1880s to 10 per cent in 1900 and peaked at nearly 20 per cent interwar, Japan supplied the bulk of her food requirements, thus conserving foreign exchange for capital goods and raw materials. As noted earlier, primary product exports, especially tea and silk, were the main foreign exchange earners until cotton and other manufactures were established. Increased agricultural output and productivity were accompanied by net migration from the land rising from about 500,000 in the decade 1875–85 to nearly 3 millions 1910–20. A marked fall to 1.2 millions 1920–30 was followed by a recovery to a peak of 7.5 millions 1955–65 [116, *246*], occasioning Kaldor's disputed remark that 'it is the existence of an elastic supply curve of labour to the secondary and tertiary sectors which is the main pre-condition of a fast rate of development'. The contribution of migrants from agriculture to increases in non-agrarian employment ranged from over 70 per cent in the 1870s to 83 per cent 1910–20 and 50 per cent in the 1930s. The percentage contribution soared again in the 1950s since when, because of the large size of the non-farm populations, it has steadily declined [116, *246*]. The secondary and tertiary sectors were tapping a huge pool of 'surplus' primary labour. Migration was partly a function of 'push' factors arising from population pressure, and of the 'lure of the city' and expectations of employment opportunities and higher wages [86, *128*].

Agriculture also released surplus 'capital' for investment in the private and public sectors but the process was far from a simple 'net transfer'. Rural landlords invested in a wide variety of non-farming enterprises such as state bonds, railways, rural industries (brewing, rice-milling, tea and silk) and banks and other financial institutions. 'Involuntary' transfers to the state via inflation-forced savings coupled with peasant taxation, especially the land-tax, were a major source of funds for the Meiji, but over time agriculture's contribution, in this as in other fields, relatively declined [148].

Preobrazhensky's concept of primitive socialist accumulation has stimulated research into intersectoral resource flows by Ishikawa [63], and Mundle and Ohkawa [94]. Conclusions remain tentative but it is confirmed that a 'savings surplus' was being transferred out of agriculture until the Second World War. On the one hand this outflow exacerbated the economic and political problems of the rural sector. On the other, agricultural savings made a positive, if only modest, contribution to capital formation in the non-agrarian private and public sectors.

Improvements in land productivity played a critical role in Japanese development until the 1920s. In particular, the fact that the real rate of growth of the basic wage good, rice, from 1880 to 1920 at 1.3 per cent per annum more than kept pace with the population growth rate of just over 1 per cent per annum, constrained rises in food prices and, therefore, in urban living costs and real wages. In turn, this facilitated the capital accumulation necessary for industrialisation.

7

Labour supply and the labour market

'Labour is the chief industrial asset of Japan. With few resources in power and raw materials, a limited supply of capital and no especial distinction in mechanical skill, Japan has built an industrial system upon cheap labour.' So wrote John Orchard [122] in 1930. Yet the emergence of a modern industrial labour force was beset with problems of recruitment, training, supply bottlenecks and inadequate managerial skills. Dorothy Orchard [121] could write in 1929 that 'labour in Japan has neither been very abundant nor very cheap for industrial purposes'. In early Meiji, ruthless exploitation, long working hours and primitive conditions are described. Female cotton and silk workers suffered low wages, a poor environment in factory and dormitory and unusually high turn-over rates. There were acute labour shortages, fierce competitive employer recruiting, sweatshops and suppression of labour movements. Over time, the dilemmas of employers and the hardships of workers were eased. The average worker in the 1930s was said to be three times better off than in the 1860s [161, *213*], and Patrick [125, *14*] thought that 'the material conditions of virtually all Japanese improved between early Meiji years and the mid-1930s'.

Labour supply is a function of changes in the participation rate, in immigration and in rates of natural increase of population. The pre-Second World War category of 'gainfully occupied workers' included self-employed and family workers as well as some unemployed. Until about 1925 the rate of growth of gainful workers at about 0.5 per cent per annum was smaller than that of population, implying a falling participation rate due, mainly, to the spread of compulsory education [116, *244*]. It accelerated from 1925 to reach a peak around 1960, an alleged turning point from 'unlimited' supplies of labour [86; 110]. Overall, any immigration was offset by emigration to the Asian empire and, peculiarly, to Brazil [151]. In 1940 98 per cent of people in Japan were ethnically Japanese [159, *64*]. The annual average population growth rate, accelerating from less than 1 per cent in early Meiji to a peak 1.4 in the interwar period, and a secular rate of about 1.2 from 1887 to 1970, was due to natural increase, an excess of births over deaths.

In the absence of an adequate census before 1920, changes in vital rates and their causes remain speculative. As was noted, the revisionist view rejects a late Tokugawa low-level equilibrium trap, postulates conscious family planning in response more to socio-economic opportunities than to disasters and finds surprisingly low but rising birth rates, with considerable regional variations. Post-1868 demographic developments were less of a transition than a continuation of Tokugawa patterns. There was a rising trend in at least crude birth rates until about 1920 with estimates of around 31 per thousand in 1870 and as high as 38 in 1920 [125, *331*]. Improved registration, a decline in abortion and accelerated economic development are among the explanations. From the 1920s we find a fertility decline, temporarily arrested in the post Second World War baby boom, and then markedly speeding up. From 1920 to 1960 crude birthrates fell from 38 to 17 and the marital general fertility rate (live legitimate births per thousand married women aged 15–49) from 218 to 108 [91]. Japanese fertility and income changes were positively related in the early stages of industrialisation and, later, beyond some critical level of income, education and urbanisation, inversely related. From the 1880s, there was a trend fall in mortality, with death rates 21 per thousand in 1890 and 7 in 1970. Today Japan claims the world's lowest infant mortality rate and one of the highest life expectancies of both men and women.

The growth of population from 34 millions in 1870 to 104 millions in 1970 was largely a result of economic development. The effect on social, political and economic change is debatable [108; 174]. Population pressure is associated with *lebensraum* and with military expansionism in the 1930s [139, *45*], but militarism may have been inherent in the ethos of Japanese nationalism. Lockwood [82, *139*] thought that 'had there been fewer people, income per capita would have been higher'; but this counterfactual ignores a positive dynamic relation between population and income growth. Kelley and Williamson [71, *137*] hypothesised considerably higher Meiji rates of population growth and found that, *ceteris paribus*, 'they would have made very little difference to her development performance'. While the size of Japan's population, especially in relation to land, had significant implications for the structure of the economy, the rate of growth was moderate compared with that in most developing countries since the Second World War.

In the context of labour supply, the Japanese dual structure is associated with theories of labour surplus and the turning point from labour surplus to labour scarcity. Most of these start from the unlimited supplies model of Lewis in which the industrial capitalist sector can expand by absorbing 'cheap' labour from the 'subsistence' sector until labour becomes relatively scarce. In the Fei–Ranis model [34; 113], until about 1920 there existed agricultural–industrial dualism, an abundant supply of unskilled labour determining and constraining real wage changes and labour-using, capital-shallowing technological progress. The turning or 'commercialisation' point was around 1920 after which the supply of surplus rural labour became limited, real wage rates rose in response to relative labour scarcity and there was substantial capital deepening. The empirical, predictive and theoretical relevance of the Fei–Ranis model and others has been exhaustively examined by Minami [86], who finds a turning point around 1960. Taira [161, *169*] warns against 'cavalier acceptance' of the unlimited supply hypothesis, and documents the formidable problems in the Meiji period 'related to the hiring, training, organisation and retention of a work-force'. The conclusion remains that industrialists were able to tap a large pool of rural labour at relatively low wages until recent years.

Fei and Ranis [113, *62*] now postulate that, while agricultural–industrial dualism disappeared after 1920, there emerged 'an intra-industrial dualism', as another reserve army made its appearance. This army was in the small-scale manufacturing and services sectors which tended to be labour-intensive with relatively low wages. In addition, while there were 'normal' wage differentials according to age, education, location, sex and skills, a much discussed [125, *201*] feature of manufacturing was the so-called 'interscale wage differential structure', a continuous spread of earnings from small to large firms. These differentials widened in the 1920s and 1930s, narrowed during the Second World War and widened again in the 1950s when they were at their maximum. In 1957 workers in establishments employing 4–9 workers were earning only 30 per cent of those in the 1000-plus group. The tightening of the labour market from the mid-1950s has attenuated both interscale and interindustry differentials.

Attempts have been made to explain this feature of the labour market in terms of capital supply, technology and factor proportions, institutions such as the seniority wage system, paternalism and other 'social' conditions [105]. The capital:labour ratio was related to scale, large firms being able to borrow more cheaply than small with better access to funds. In addition, technological constraints and the rigidity of factor proportions, especially in heavy industries relying on foreign technology, limited the substitutability of labour for capital, dictating relatively capital-intensive techniques, high productivity and high wages. In so far as the technology was specific to a particular firm, it *had* to pay high wages and give permanent employment in order to retain skilled workers. Where technology was less specific and could diffuse more readily as in the case of cotton textiles, there was mobility of workers between firms and relatively small wage-differentials. Monopolistic control over product prices also permitted the payment of higher wages by oligopolistic groups who were developing in heavy industry in the 1920s when the wage differential was amplifying. Other explanations have been sought in 'institutional' factors, prominently the permanent employment, *nenkō-joretsu* (seniority wage) system. It resulted in segmented labour markets and reduced wage-equalising interfirm labour mobility. Yasuba [125, *285*] maintains that low-wage workers in small-scale industries received compensation in close personal relations and paternalistic contact. As companies grew bigger and more complex, there was increasing separation between ownership, management and employees, offset by larger firms institutionalising a new kind of paternalism providing higher wages, assured employment and fringe benefits. The preferential position of big company workers was reinforced by trade unions. There was no adequate system of nationwide collective bargaining to improve the status of small-scale workers and 'the logic of enterprise unionism works for the widening of wage differentials between large and smaller firms' [160, *203*].

Japan avoided the 'labour-absorption problem', common now in many developing countries. Rapid industrialisation ensured a burgeoning demand for labour and a continuing reallocation of labour from the relatively low-productivity agrarian and small-industry sectors to the high-productivity modern manufacturing sector. Wage differentials also allowed a wide range of factor combinations, given that there was sufficient demand for both 'traditional' and 'modern' products.

The contribution of labour to growth is not only a function of numbers and absorption, but also of statistically elusive quality improvements. It is not easy to separate myth from reality in that most widespread of all generalisations about Japanese workers, from Veblen [167, *284*] to Vogel [169, *131*] that, especially compared with those in the West, they were dedicated, diligent, disciplined, loyal 'workaholics' [165]. Growth-accounting studies attribute quality betterment less to variations in age and sex, and increased effort due to health and nutrition, and more to advances in education. Japanese workers are now among the most literate and the most numerate in the world.

Panegyrists of the Japanese success story look not only to the high quality and elastic supply of 'cheap' labour but also to the organisation of the labour market and industrial relations [24; 105; 119; 141]. The three and sometimes four 'treasures' or 'pillars' of the Japanese system were seniority wages, permanent employment or lifetime commitment, enterprise unions and conflict-avoiding, collective decision-making. The extent, uniqueness, origins, efficiency and future of the system have been scrutinised in an enormous literature, by those who see it as an anachronistic symptom of the immaturity of capitalism and by those who wish that it could be transplanted to the West [37].

Under the 'pure' seniority wage or *nenkō* system, wages are related not to productivity or economic efficiency but to personal factors such as education, length of service and age. The 'white-collarisation' hypothesis of Koike [144, *29*] likens the steep age-wage profile of Japanese blue-collar workers to that of white-collar workers in the West, a development arising from the growth of large monopolistic firms in the industrialisation process. Employees also receive twice yearly negotiable bonuses, supplementary allowances and fringe benefits including facilities for canteens, education, health and sports. A lump sum payment is made on compulsory retirement at the age of 55. Permanent employment implies the hiring of workers directly from school or college, thereafter with tenure until the retiring age. Discharge, temporary lay-offs and premature resignation are rare. Both employers and employees have a reciprocal lifetime commitment to the enterprise. A stable homogeneous workforce guaranteed security and rising earnings to meet family needs ensures identification with the company's goals. There are no accurate data on the extent of the institution which arose soon after the First World War and became widespread after the second. Both *nenkō* and *shūshin koyo* (lifetime employment) are more or less exclusive to large-scale modern private enterprises and the public sector. Women are generally outside the arrangement and all firms have a substantial proportion of casual or temporary workers liable to lay-off. Levine [83, *661*] estimated that in 1960 under 45 per cent of non-agricultural wage-earners were covered by the *nenkō* system, and Cole [20] disputes its uniqueness.

Origins have been ascribed variously to the welfare corporatism of a late developer, to deep-rooted socio-cultural factors and to rational responses to economic change. Abegglen [1] in the 'classical cultural approach', postulates a carry-over of pre-industrial family and paternalistic structures. Relations between employer and employee are not explicable in formal contractual terms. 'The enterprise is the people' and the traditional *ie* (family) have been adapted to the modern enterprise as in the 'One Railway Family' (*kokutetsu-ikka*) of Japanese National Railways. There is now more support for Taira's [160] view that the system was an 'institutional invention' by rational employers to offset labour market costs of recruitment, inadequate skills and difficulties in retaining trained workers. The system grew sporadically in the interwar period and only became predominant after the Second World War, further suggesting that a cultural legacy was less significant than the rational, profit-maximising behaviour of employers exploiting changes in the labour market.

The economic efficiency of the arrangement is not self-evident. Where wages are more or less a fixed cost and employers are unable to dismiss workers, inflexibility in depressions would appear a severe burden. However, all firms carried a substantial number of women and temporary workers who could be laid-off. In addition relatively early retirement reduced costs. Perhaps most important, the prevalence of subcontracting meant that the employment repercussions of slack demand were borne, not by the parent company, but by the subcontractor and his employees. Moreover such costs as arose from the wage and employment system were further outweighed by the other two 'pillars', enterprise unionism and group decision-making.

Some western capitalists have looked with envy at the weakness of the Japanese trade union movement before the Second World War and at the submissive and cooperative nature of enterprise unions thereafter. Apart from a brief upsurge in the 1920s under the 'Taisho democracy', the unions before 1940 were severely repressed and never legitimised [79]. Peak membership in 1936 was only 420,000, much of it in enterprise unions, and the rate of unionisation in all manufacturing industries in the 1930s was between 5 and 8 per cent of workers [160, *144*]. After the war the American democratisation drive included the growth of a 'free' trade union movement. Membership grew rapidly to encompass 33 per cent of all employees by 1973 [126, *628*]. Late-developing Japan escaped the entrenched craft and industrial unions of Britain. In 1975 some 83 per cent of union members and 94 per cent of unions were of the enterprise form [144, *117*]. Membership is restricted to regular employees of an individual company or enterprise, blue- and white-collar workers are in the same union, decisions are taken at the local level and loyalties are confined to the firm rather than to occupations, crafts or classes. While the system does not prevent strikes, these are usually of short duration, are most common in the spring wage-offensive, and have been likened to 'a ritualistic fist-shaking', with action falling short of measures that would seriously damage the company [126, *646*].

In addition to seniority wages, permanent employment and enterprise unions, the OECD [123] distinguished a further, fourth 'pillar' in terms of the social norms within a company. These included cooperation between management and workers in the interests of the 'family' enterprise and an elaborate system of group, consensual decision-making and joint consultation at all levels. Prolonged discussions precede a decision but, once agreed, it is rapidly implemented. Most important in the view of Glazer [126, *887*] was the egalitarian nature of factory society, the lack of distinction in speech, dress, eating facilities and class, the whole system allegedly resulting in 'conflict-avoidance' [43].

There are obvious advantages to employers in the Japanese institution. In particular, while interenterprise labour mobility may be limited, the allocation of labour within firms is highly flexible, unhampered by craft demarcation problems and conducive to rapid technical change. Workers embraced by the arrangements also gain from job security in the face of labour-saving innovation, steady wage rises no matter what their occupation and the status and perks of company membership. There are, however, plenty of criticisms of the system as it operates and doubts about its future viability. Skinner [150] queries the reality of group decision-making and absence of conflict and Tokunaga's [144, *313*] Marxist interpretation points to the 'emasculation' of trade unions and their inability to influence managerial policy. As was noted, also, the majority of Japanese workers remain outside the system thus perpetuating the dualistic structure. In recent years efficiency-related earnings have brought modifications to seniority wages and there is a view that lifetime commitment would not survive a prolonged depression. Galenson and Odaka [126, *670*] believe that 'movement towards a Western labor market model is optimal for the future stability of Japan'. Others such as Dore [30] see convergence towards the allegedly superior Japanese practices. Human resources [81] were Japan's chief asset and the industrial relations system with all its defects made a major contribution to their productive utilisation in the industrialisation process.

8
Capital, technology and enterprise

Industrialisation requires increasing capital formation to provide assets to keep pace with the growth in labour, to raise productivity by substituting capital for labour and to allow 'embodied' technical progress. In growth-accounting terms the 'contribution' of the growth rate of gross capital stock to the rate of growth of output was invariably much higher than that of labour. While Japan used traditional labour-intensive techniques where appropriate and adapted western technology to suit her factor endowments and prices, modern industrialisation necessitated modern technology and that presupposes a fast rate of capital accumulation.

From the 1880s to the 1930s, the ratio of gross domestic capital formation to GNP rose from 12 to 25 per cent and the ratio of net domestic capital formation to NNP from 8 to 20 per cent, most of the increases having taken place in the interwar period [134, 9]. A structural decomposition of gross domestic fixed capital formation demonstrates that the rise in producers' durables from under 18 per cent in the 1880s to 60 per cent in 1938 was the key to trend acceleration in industrial growth [116, 27]. Since the Second World War the high productivity of capital stock is evinced by a relatively low and falling capital:output ratio due to rapid technical progress and a consequent relatively young age of capital. The prewar incremental capital:output ratio was higher and a slight secular trend rise is evident. Capital-deepening or a rise in the capital:labour ratio was also a feature. Between 1885 and 1940 the aggregate capital:labour (K/L) ratio in yen per gainfully employed person rose more than 5 times from 322 to 1772 [116, 189].

How and why Japanese entrepreneurs invested so high a proportion of their income and whence came the savings have aroused much discussion. Autonomous investment associated with technical progress and imitative innovations stimulated growth in incomes and consumption which, in turn, led to induced capital formation. A high inducement to invest was sustained by the high realised and expected profits accompanying trend acceleration in growth, reinforced by the status awarded by 'up-to-dateness' [102, 95]. Generally 'docile' workers and lags between wages and productivity favoured employers. While military outlays may have crowded-out some private investment, state policies stimulated entrepreneurial expectations through a generally expansionary monetary stance and a fiscal system in which in 1930 income taxes contributed only 14 per cent and business taxes 8 per cent to central government tax take.

Demand for capital had to be matched by the savings to finance it. Since the Second World War Japan's ratio of gross domestic savings to GNP (40 per cent in 1970) has been higher than that in the USA and EEC [11, *84;* 149, *20*]. Before the war the ratio rose from 13 per cent in 1880 to 22 per cent in 1938 [116, *30*]. Despite a large and growing deficit between government revenues and current expenditures and consistently high public sector absorption, private savings were also remarkable. These are conventionally divided into corporate and personal or household savings. Corporate savings accounted for only 2 or 3 per cent of all domestic savings before 1930 and 10 per cent in the late 1930s. While some of the sources were reploughing of after-tax profits and there were big rates of depreciation, most striking was the reliance on external funds. Corporate financing is characterised by an unusually low ratio of equity to total capitalisation, by heavy reliance on trade credit and by high levels of bank borrowing occasioning the much used phrases 'overborrowing' and 'overlending' [126, *267*].

Personal savings in Japan are now claimed to be the highest of any major country [126, *256*]. Before the war, personal or household savings accounted for as much as 56 per cent of all domestic savings in peak year 1917 and 41 per cent in 1937 [114, *168*]. There is a variety of interconnected social, economic and institutional interpretations. Thriftiness has been noted as a major Tokugawa legacy. Thunberg [162, *III, 257*], commented in 1776 that 'frugality has its principal seat in Japan. It is a virtue as highly esteemed in the imperial palace as in the poorest cottage.' Comparisons have been made between Confucian and Victorian Calvinistic stress on diligence and thrift [72]. The main cause of increasing savings was the rapid rate of economic growth but, given that the average level of per capita income was much lower than in the West, additional explanations are required. These include the possibility that rapid growth ensured that actual incomes were higher than the expected 'permanent incomes' on which consumption decisions were based. Income inequalities have some relevance for the interwar period but since the Second World War income distribution is probably less skewed than that in other OECD countries [11, 86].

Structural and institutional factors have been invoked, such as the high share in income and employment of unincorporated enterprises and self-employed farmers. Included in personal and household, the *a priori* case that precautionary and investment motives would give them higher than average savings propensities is empirically verified. The demographic structure had a bias towards the saving young and middle-aged group and against older dis-savers. The absence of a 'welfare state' required households to save for education and possible sickness and unemployment. Incentives to save may also have been incited by lack of credit facilities for consumer durables and housing and, in so far as the amounts were in excess of expectations, by twice-yearly bonus windfall payments to factory workers. The development of financial institutions such as banks, cooperative credit societies and post office savings arrangements encouraged the mobilisation of existing savings but their role in creating new savings is more doubtful and Japan lacked the wider lending choices available in western bond markets. Moderate secular inflation and relatively low real interest rates had both positive and negative effects on savings with their overall impact uncertain [126, 261]. Japan's exceptionally high savings rates were the result of an unusual willingness to abstain from consumption and an ability to save which was largely a function of economic growth, itself due to investment and accompanying technical progress.

Japan, unlike eighteenth-century Britain, was noted neither for original research nor for inventions, a fact deplored by Count Okuma [120, *II*, *565*]. The syndrome is one of borrowing, imitating, adapting and organising foreign technology, of exploiting the technological gap. It has a long history and still continues. Tokugawa isolationism restricted but did not entirely prevent some absorption of overseas ideas and goods such as the telescope depicted in a 1682 print of a man on a rooftop watching a lady bathing. Attempts have been made to measure technical imports through royalty payments. These are only rough guides, as are data which show a rise in the share of chemicals, metals and machinery in imports in current prices from 21 per cent in the 1870s to 75 per cent in the 1930s and a peak 89 per cent in the late 1950s [116, *137*]. Modern Japan had the desire to import technology and the means to pay for it through export earnings. However, as Peck [126, *581*] says, she went further than the rhetoric of American officials and of Harold Wilson's 'white hot technical revolution', and actually achieved the application of technology for economic growth.

How this achievement was realised raises complex issues of trial and error, of learning by doing, of socio-institutional absorptive capacity, and of adaptation to factor endowments [54]. Early on, there was a good deal of slavish imitation, as in Lockwood's [82, *332*] description of the tailor copying 'the Western suit of clothes even to the patch on the pants'. Failures in design and operation were common. It is said that railway engines blew up through lack of water and Tipton [163] is cynical about Meiji government attempts to introduce new technology. What is remarkable is not that ineptness and disasters marked initial efforts to use alien techniques but that Japan so soon developed the 'social capability' to import technology [114, *218*]. Two aspects of this 'social capability' were the creation of an environment conducive to the widespread diffusion of technology and more or less successful attempts to 'japanise' it. From the early Meiji to the post-Second World War Ministry of International Trade and Industry, the role of government was significant both indirectly in encouraging a climate of growth and directly through more active economic and institutional measures. In the private sector the more spectacular changes were promoted by the *zaibatsu* groups which had the size to achieve scale economies, the managerial acumen to organise efficiently a non-Luddite labour force, the diversification to install a wide range of techniques and, in their financial affiliates, the ability to mobilise capital. But, as Inkster [61] points out, Schumpeterian innovative 'leaps and bounds' are not the whole story. Farmers and small manufacturers were experimenting and choosing techniques which were appropriate for climate, location and factor endowments.

There is debate about factor proportions and whether techniques were capital- or labour-intensive [10]. In fact, we find a wide spectrum of techniques, corresponding to different factor costs, ranging from the sophisticated best-practice machines of some modern firms to small electric motors in workshops. Ono [113, *236*] distinguishes between 'adapted' and 'non-adapted' borrowed technology. The former tended to be more suitable for Japanese relative factor endowments and included some early private ironworks and, most notably, the raw silk industry. 'Non-adapted' technology was more capital-intensive and is evident in the government-run Kamaishi and Yawata ironworks, which imported advanced equipment with little modification. Although foreigners neither ran industry nor directly imposed their western methods on it, Japanese reliance on foreign technology, not to mention military requirements, constrained the choice of techniques and dictated capital-intensive methods in the modern sector. In the 'traditional' small-scale sector of the dual economy more labour-intensive methods were feasible. Rigidities in factor proportions could be reduced by 'mitigation techniques' [114, *90*]. For example an early strategy based on indigenous sectors, such as peasant farming and raw silk, needed neither large capital outlays nor foreign exchange. Relatively scarce capital could be economised by multi-shift working, by the use of second-hand machines, and by subcontracting some operations to labour-intensive small-scale enterprises.

All this presupposes an adequate supply of aggressive, entrepreneurial managers and businessmen with high 'animal spirits' [73; 96]. There were good and bad entrepreneurs and managers and 'objectivity in the evaluation of entrepreneurial achievement is difficult to attain' [157, *255*]. At the Restoration private entrepreneurship was relatively scarce in new fields, an alleged reason for the state's pioneering role, and the successful, partly with government support, were able to monopolise sectors of modern industry. This élite, epitomised in the *zaibatsu*, are depicted both as the main promoters of modern economic growth with all its benefits and as the exploiting 'robber barons' who perpetuated the dual structure, who exemplify Lenin's 'Highest Stage of Capitalism', who provoked the democratising American authorities to dissolve them and rose again, phoenix-like, although in somewhat emasculated and different guise. Yamamura [178] takes issue with the 'orthodox' view of Ranis [129] and Hirschmeier [56] that at least early Japanese entrepreneurs were peculiar because they were mainly *Samurai*, imbued with the spirit of that class, not motivated mainly by personal profit but acting in a 'community-centred' way for the enrichment of the nation. His study of the origins of entrepreneurs finds both that class categorisations are blurred and that many were of humble origin and inspired by desire for profit. It remains true, however, that in a 'capitalist' society, the pace of economic growth is basically determined by the amount and quality of entrepreneurial and managerial activity and that Japanese economic success in itself testifies to the abundance of that factor.

9
Conclusion

Despite the abundance of statistics and interpretations, explanations of how Japan 'did it' remain elusive. Growth was a function of a large number of peculiar interacting non-economic and economic factors, all of which were necessary conditions but none alone sufficient. We find elements of both the Weberian syndrome where the ethos determines the economy and of the Marxist where material conditions influence society. Two fundamental conditions for modern economic growth were the 'Tokugawa legacy' and the role of the government. The contribution of the former in the socio-cultural fields, in attitudes to thrift, diligence and loyalty, has long been recognised, but it is only in recent years that the extent of economic development before 1868 is becoming fully appreciated. The role of the government was crucial, not so much in terms of pioneering industries and taxes and subsidies, but in its moulding of society to conform to its military and therefore economic objectives. Toynbee's concept of challenge and response is illuminating. Perry's black ships symbolise the challenge of possible western colonisation. The response was not to withdraw further into an isolationist posture but to emulate and catch up with the West. This required both a radical transformation of some socio-economic institutions and the strengthening of traditional nationalistic values through state Shintoism and educational propaganda. Political independence enabled Japan to control some of the potentially damaging aspects of western modernisation and to indulge in eclecticism in borrowing from abroad. Compared with, say, India, the relative homogeneity of language and society facilitated state direction. The response to the western challenge was *fukoku kyohei*, rich country, strong army. The route to the former was a mixture of absolutism and modern capitalism. The logical outcome of the latter was imperialistic expansionism and war culminating in Pearl Harbour.

Students of economic development tend to concentrate on the mechanism by which a relatively late starter successively exploited the opportunities arising from backwardness. This involved a complex interplay of demand and supply conditions. Although consumption growth was constrained, the rapid expansion of the internal market supplemented by overseas demand provided an environment of accelerating private investment and technical innovation, much of it imported. On the supply side, the ability to tap world markets overcame a possible raw material bottleneck and the development of indigenous agriculture provided the growing population with basic necessities. The abundant supply factor was human resources, a relatively elastic supply of good-quality labour and enterprising businessmen and managers. Capital remained scarce but, without large recourse to foreign savings, not only was a fast rate of capital accumulation achieved but more or less capital- and labour-intensive techniques were accommodated to a wide range of differential factor costs.

These processes were not painless. There were considerable regional and class variations in performance and rewards. There were, within trend acceleration, phases of rapid and slow growth and economic crises, especially in the 1920s. In particular, much of the literature stresses the costs of giving primacy to military and economic advance in terms of the environment, real wages, the standard of living and welfare. It should be remembered, however, that the material conditions of most Japanese showed substantial absolute improvement over time as a result of economic growth. It is at least arguable whether different strategies with less emphasis on development and expansionism and more on consumption and social needs would have benefited the majority of Japanese.

Bibliography

The literature on Japanese economic history in English, Japanese and other languages is enormous and growing rapidly. A sample of research in Japanese is available in Sumiya and Taira [157] and in Yonekawa [180]. Bibliographies include that being compiled by the Institute of Developing Economies (Tada) [158] and the annual *Bibliography of Asian Studies* published by the Association of Asian Studies (Ann Arbor, Michigan). The items listed below comprise only a small selection of works in English of which Beasley [7], Ohkawa and Rosovsky [114] and Patrick and Rosovsky [126] are notable.

[1] Abegglen, J. C. (1958) *The Japanese Factory: Aspects of its Social Organisation* (Glencoe, Free Press).

[2] Akamatsu, K. (1962) 'A Historical Pattern of Economic Growth in Developing Countries', *The Developing Economies* (March–August).

[3] Allen, G. C. (1962) *A Short Economic History of Modern Japan* (London, Allen and Unwin).

[4] Allen, G. C. (1981) *The Japanese Economy* (London, Weidenfeld and Nicolson).

[5] Anderson, R. S. (1975) *Education in Japan: A Century of Modern Development* (Washington, US Government Printing Office).

[6] Austin, L. (1976) *The Paradox of Progress* (Yale).

[7] Beasley, W. G. (1981) *The Modern History of Japan* (London, Weidenfeld and Nicolson).

[8] Bieda, K. (1979) *The Structure and Operation of the Japanese Economy* (Sydney, Wiley).

[9] Bird, R. M. (1977) 'Land Taxation and Economic Development in Meiji Japan', *Journal of Development Studies*, 13, no. 2 (January).

[10] Blumenthal, T. (1980) 'Factor Proportions and Choice of Technology; the Japanese Experience', *Economic Development and Cultural*

Change, 28, no. 3 (April) and (1981)'Comment' by Fei and Ranis, 29, no. 4 (July).

[11] Boltho, A. (1975) *Japan. An Economic Survey 1953–1973* (Oxford).

[12] Boulding, K. E. and Gleason, A. H. (1972) 'War as an Investment. The Strange Case of Japan' in K. E. Boulding and T. Mukerjee (eds), *Economic Imperialism* (Ann Arbor).

[13] Bowen, R. W. (1980) *Rebellion and Democracy in Meiji Japan. A Study of Commoners in the Popular Rights Movement* (Berkeley).

[14] Broadbridge, S. (1974) 'Economic and Social Trends in Tokugawa Japan', *Modern Asian Studies*, 8, no. 3.

[15] Broadbridge, S. (1976) *Industrial Dualism in Japan* (London, Frank Cass).

[16] Burks, A. W. (ed.) (1985) *The Modernizers: Overseas Students, Foreign Employees and Meiji Japan* (Boulder and London, Westview Press).

[17] Caves, R. E. (1971) 'Export-led Growth and the New Economic History' in J. N. Bhagwati (ed.), *Trade, Balance of Payments and Growth* (Amsterdam).

[18] Caves, R. E. and Uekusa, M. (1976) *Industrial Organisation in Japan* (Washington, The Brookings Institution).

[19] Clark, R. (1979) *The Japanese Company* (Yale).

[20] Cole, R. E. (1978) 'The Late-Developer Hypothesis: an Examination of its Relevance for Japanese Employment Practices', *Journal of Japanese Studies*, 4, no. 2 (Summer).

[21] Cowan, C. D. (ed.) (1964) *The Economic Development of China and Japan* (London, Allen and Unwin).

[22] Craig, A. M. (ed.) (1979) *Japan. A Comparative View* (Princeton).

[23] Crawcour, S. (1974) 'The Tokugawa Period and Japan's Preparation for Modern Economic Growth', *Journal of Japanese Studies*, 1, no. 1 (Autumn).

[24] Crawcour, S. (1978) 'The Japanese Employment System', *Journal of Japanese Studies*, 4, no. 2 (Summer).

[25] Cummings, W. K. (1980) *Education and Equality in Japan* (Princeton).

[26] Daniels, G. (ed.) (1984) *Europe Interprets Japan* (Tenterden, Norbury).

[27] Denison, E. F. and Chung, W. K. (1976) *How Japan's Economy Grew So Fast. The Sources of Postwar Expansion* (Washington, The Brookings Institution).

[28] Dore, R. P. (1959) *Land Reform in Japan* (Oxford).

[29] Dore, R. P. (ed.) (1971) *Aspects of Social Change in Modern Japan* (Princeton).

[30] Dore, R. P. (1973) *British Factory – Japanese Factory. The Origins of National Diversity in Industrial Relations* (London, Allen and Unwin).

[31] Dore, R. P. (1984) *Education in Tokugawa Japan* (London, Athlone).

[32] Dore, R. P. (1985) *Flexible Rigidities, Industrial Policy and Structural Adjustment in the Japanese Economy, 1970–1980* (London, Athlone).

[33] Dower, J. W. (1975) *Origins of the Modern Japanese State. Selected Writings of E.H. Norman* (New York, Random House).

[34] Fei, J. C. H. and Ranis, G. (1964) *Development of a Labour Surplus Economy: Theory and Policy* (Homewood, Illinois, Irwin).

[35] Francks, P. (1984) *Technology and Agricultural Development in Pre-war Japan* (Yale).

[36] Frank, A. G. (1978) *Dependent Accumulation and Underdevelopment* (London, Macmillan).

[37] Fruin, W. M. (1978) 'The Japanese Company Controversy', *Journal of Japanese Studies*, 4, no. 2 (Summer).

[38] Gluck, C. (1978) 'The People in History. Recent Trends in Japanese Historiography', *Journal of Asian Studies*, 38, no. 1 (November).

[39] Goldsmith, R. W. (1983) *The Financial Development of India, Japan and the United States* (Yale).

[40] Goldsmith, R. W. (1983) *The Financial Development of Japan 1868–1977* (Yale).

[41] Golovnin, V. M. (1819) *Recollections of Japan* (London).

[42] Goodman, G. K. (1985) *Japan, the Dutch Experience* (London, Athlone).

[43] Gordon, R. J. (1982) 'Why U.S. Wage and Employment Behaviour differs from that in Britain and Japan', *Economic Journal*, 92 (March).

[44] Grabowski R. (1985) 'A Historical Reassessment of Early Japanese Development', *Development and Change*, 16, no. 2 (April).

[45] Grabowski, R. and Sivan, D. (1983) 'The Direction of Technological Change in Japanese Agriculture, 1874–1971', *The Developing Economies*, 21, no. 3 (September).

[46] Grabowski, R. and Yoon, B. J. (1984) 'Intersectoral Terms of Trade, Industrial Labour Supply and the Classical Model: early Japanese Experience', *The Developing Economies*, 22, no. 3 (September).

[47] Hall, J. W. and Jansen, M. B. (1968) *Studies in the Institutional History of Early Modern Japan* (Princeton).

[48] Halliday, J. (1975) *A Political History of Japanese Capitalism* (London, Monthly Review Press).

[49] Hanley, S. B. (1983) 'A High Standard of Living in Nineteenth Century Japan: Fact or Fantasy?', *Journal of Economic History*, 43, no. 1 (March).

[50] Hanley, S. B. and Yamamura, K. (1977) *Economic and Demographic Change in Pre-industrial Japan, 1600–1868* (Princeton).

[51] Hauser, W. B. (1974) *Economic Institutional Change in Tokugawa Japan* (Cambridge).

[52] Hayami, A. (1980) 'Class Differences in Marriage and Fertility

among Tokugawa Villagers in Mino Province', *Keio Economic Studies*. 17.

[53] Hayami, Y. (1975) *A Century of Agricultural Growth in Japan* (Tokyo).

[54] Hayashi, T. *et al.* (1979) 'Technological Transfer and Adaptation: the Japanese Experience', *The Developing Economies* (special issue), 17, no. 4 (December).

[55] Hidetoshi, K. (1981) 'The Significance of the Period of National Seclusion reconsidered', *Journal of Japanese Studies*, 7, no. 1 (Winter).

[56] Hirschmeier, J. and Yui, T. (1981) *The Development of Japanese Business* (London, Allen and Unwin).

[57] Hollerman, L. (1981) 'A Sampling of Japanese Economic Issues', *Journal of Asian Studies*, 40 no. 4 (August).

[58] Horie, Y. (1956) 'Problems of the Modernisation of Japan', Kyoto University Economic Review, 26, no. 1 (April).

[59] Hoston, G. A. (1984) 'Marxism and National Socialism in Taisho Japan. The Thought of Takabatake Motoyuki', *Journal of Asian Studies*, 44, no. 1 (November).

[60] Huber, T. M. (1981) *The Revolutionary Origins of Modern Japan* (Stanford).

[61] Inkster, I. (1979) 'Meiji Economic Development in Perspective; Revisionist Comments upon the Industrial Revolution in Japan', *The Developing Economies*, 17, no. 1 (March). Also (1977) *Journal of Economic History*, 37, no. 4 (December).

[62] Inkster, I. (1980) *Japan as a Development Model. Relative Backwardness and Technological Transfer* (Bochum, Studienverlag).

[63] Ishikawa, S. (1967) *Economic Development in Asian Perspective* (Tokyo, Kinokuniya).

[64] Ishikawa, S. (1981) *Essays on Technology, Employment and Institutions in Economic Development* (Tokyo, Kinokuniya).

[65] Jansen, M. B. (ed.) (1965) *Changing Japanese Attitudes toward Modernisation* (Princeton).

[66] Johnson, C. (1982) *M.I.T.I. and the Japanese Miracle. The Growth of Industrial Policy 1925–1975* (Stanford).

[67] Jones, H. J. (1980) *Live Machines, Hired Foreigners and Meiji Japan* (Vancouver, University of British Columbia).

[68] Kaempfer, E. (1906) *The History of Japan, together with a Description of the Kingdom of Siam. 1690–92* (Glasgow, MacLehose).

[69] Kahn, H. (1973) *The Emerging Japanese Superstate* (Pelican).

[70] Keene, D. (1969) *The Japanese Discovery of Europe* (Stanford).

[71] Kelley, A. C. and Williamson, J. G. (1974) *Lessons from Japanese Development. An Analytical Economic History* (Chicago).

[72] Kinmonth, E. H. (1981) *The Self-Made Man in Meiji Japanese Thought: from Samurai to Salary Man* (Berkeley).

[73] Kiyokawa, Y. (1984) 'Entrepreneurship and Innovation in Japan', *The Developing Economies* 22, no. 3 (September).

[74] Klein, L. and Ohkawa, K. (1968) *Economic Growth. The Japanese Experience since the Meiji Era* (Homewood, Illinois, Irwin).

[75] Koh, S. J. (1966) *Stages of Industrial Development in Asia. A Comparative History of the Cotton Industry in Japan, India, China and Korea* (Oxford).

[76] Kravis, I. B., Heston, A. W. and Summers, R. (1978) 'Real GDP per capita for more than one hundred countries', *Economic Journal*, 88, no. 350 (June). Also (1978) *U.N. International Comparison Project: Phase II. International Comparisons of Real Product and Purchasing Power* (Johns Hopkins).

[77] Kuznets, S. (1971) *Economic Growth of Nations. Total Output and Production Structure* (Harvard).

[78] Kuznets, S., Moore, W. E. and Spengler, J. J. (eds) (1955) *Economic growth: Brazil, India, Japan* (Duke).

[79] Large, S. S. (1981) *Organised Workers and Socialist Politics in Interwar Japan* (Cambridge).

[80] Lehmann, J.-P. (1982) *The Roots of Modern Japan* (London, Macmillan).

[81] Levine, S. B. and Kawada, H. (1980) *Human Resources in Japanese Industrial Development* (Princeton).

[82] Lockwood, W. W. (1955) *The Economic Development of Japan. Growth and Structural Change 1868–1938* (Oxford).

[83] Lockwood, W. W. (ed.) (1965) *The State and Economic Enterprise in Japan* (Princeton).

[84] Macpherson, W. J. (1972) 'Economic Development in India under the British Crown, 1858–1947', in A. J. Youngson (ed.), *Economic Development in the Long Run* (London, Allen and Unwin).

[85] Magaziner, I. C. and Hunt, T. M. (1980) *Japanese Industrial Policy* (Berkeley).

[86] Minami, R. (1973) *The Turning Point in Economic Development. Japan's Experience* (Tokyo, Kinokuniya).

[87] Minami, R. and Ono, A. (1981) 'Behaviour of Income Shares in a Labour-Surplus Economy', *Economic Development and Cultural Change*, 29, no. 2 (January).

[88] Moore, R. Barrington, (1973) *Social Origins of Dictatorship and Democracy* (Harmondsworth, Penguin).

[89] Morishima, M. (1982) *Why has Japan 'Succeeded'? Western Technology and the Japanese Ethos* (Cambridge).

[90] Morley, J. W. (ed.) (1971) *Dilemmas of Growth in Prewar Japan* (Princeton).

[91] Mosk, C. (1977) 'Demographic Transition in Japan', *Journal of Economic History*, 37, no. 3 (September).

[92] Mosk, C. (1981) 'The Evolution of the Pre-Modern Demographic Regime in Japan', *Population Studies*, 35, no. 1 (March).

[93] Moulder, F. V. (1979) *Japan, China and the Modern World Economy* (Cambridge).

[94] Mundle, S. and Ohkawa, K. (1979) 'Agricultural and Surplus Flow in Japan, 1888–1937', *The Developing Economies*, 17, no. 3 (September).

[95] Myers, R. H. and Peattie, M. R. (eds) (1984) *The Japanese Colonial Empire*, 1895–1945 (Princeton).

[96] Nakagawa, K. *et al.* (eds) (1976) *Strategy and Structure of Big Business*; (1977) *Social Order and Entrepreneurship*; (1978) *Marketing and Finance in the Course of Industrialisation*; (1979) *Labour and Management*; (1980) *Development and Diffusion of Technology*; (1980) *Development of Mass Marketing: the Automobile and Retailing Industries*; (1982) *Textile Industry and its Business Climate*; (1984) *Overseas Business Activities*. (Proceedings of Fuji Conferences, Tokyo University Press.)

[97] Nakamura, J. I. (1966) *Agricultural Production and the Economic Development of Japan* (Princeton).

[98] Nakamura, J. I. (1981) 'Human Capital Accumulation in Pre-Modern Rural Japan', *Journal of Economic History*, 41, no. 2 (June).

[99] Nakamura, J. I. and Miyamoto, M. (1982) 'Social Structure and Population Change. A Comparative Study of Tokugawa Japan and Ch'ing China', *Economic Development and Cultural Change*, 30, no. 2 (January).

[100] Nakamura, T. (1981) *The Postwar Japanese Economy. Its Development and Structure* (Tokyo).

[101] Nakamura, T. (1983) *Economic growth in pre-war Japan* (Yale).

[102] Nakane, C. (1979) *Japanese Society* (Harmondsworth, Penguin).

[103] Nghiep, L. T. (1979) 'The Structure and Change in Technology in Pre-war Japanese Agriculture', *American Journal of Agricultural Economics*, 61, no. 4 (November).

[104] Nish, I. and Dunn, C. (eds) (1979) *European Studies on Japan* (Tenterden, Kent, Norbury).

[105] Nishikawa, S. (ed.) (1980) *The Labor Market in Japan* (Tokyo, The Japan Foundation).

[106] Norman, E. H. (1940) *Japan's Emergence as a Modern State* (New York, Institute of Pacific Relations).

[107] Nurkse, R. (1953) *Problems of Capital Formation in Underdeveloped Countries* (Oxford, Blackwell).

[108] Ogawa, N. and Suits, D. B. (1982) 'Lessons of Population and

Economic Change from Meiji Experience', *The Developing Econo-mies*, 20, no. 2 (June).

[109] Ohkawa, K. (1957) *The Growth-rate of the Japanese Economy since 1878* (Tokyo, Kinokuniya).

[110] Ohkawa, K. (1972) *Differential Structure and Agriculture. Essays on Dualistic Growth* (Tokyo, Kinokuniya).

[111] Ohkawa, K. and Hayami, Y. (eds) (1973) *Economic Growth. The Japanese Experience since the Meiji Era* (Tokyo, Japan Economic Research Center).

[112] Ohkawa, K., Johnston, B. F. and Kaneda, H. (eds) (1969) *Agricul-ture and Economic Growth. Japan's Experience* (Princeton).

[113] Ohkawa, K. and Ranis, G. (eds) (1985) *Japan and the Developing Countries* (Oxford, Blackwell).

[114] Ohkawa, K. and Rosovsky, H. (1973) *Japanese Economic Growth. Trend Acceleration in the Twentieth Century* (Stanford).

[115] Ohkawa, K. and Rosovsky, H. (1978) 'Capital Formation in Japan', *Cambridge Economic History of Europe* (Cambridge), vol. VII, part 2, ch. III.

[116] Ohkawa, K. and Shinohara, M. (eds) (1979) *Patterns of Japanese Economic Development. A Quantitative Appraisal* (Yale).

[117] Ohkawa, K., Shinohara, M. and Umemura, M. (eds) 1965–) *Estimates of Long-Term Economic Statistics of Japan* (Tokyo, Toyo Keizai Shimposha, 14 volumes).

[118] Okita, S. (1980) *The Developing Economies and Japan. Lessons in Growth* (Tokyo).

[119] Okochi, K., Karsh, B. and Levine, S. B. (eds) (1973) *Workers and Employers in Japan: the Japanese Employment Relations System* (Princeton).

[120] Okuma, S. (ed.) (1909) *Fifty Years of New Japan* (London).

[121] Orchard, D. K. (1929) 'An Analysis of Japan's Cheap Labour', *Political Science Quarterly*, 44, no. 2 (June).

[122] Orchard, J. E. (1930) *Japan's Economic Position. The Progress of Industrialisation* (New York, Whittlesey).

[123] Organisation for Economic Cooperation and Development (1977) *The Development of Industrial Relations Systems: Some Implications of Japanese Experience* (Paris).

[124] Oshima, H. T. (1982) 'Reinterpreting Japan's Post-War Growth', *Economic Development and Cultural Change*, 31, no. 1 (October).

[125] Patrick, H. (ed.) (1976) *Japanese Industrialisation and its Social Consequences* (Berkeley).

[126] Patrick, H. and Rosovsky, H. (eds) (1976) *Asia's New Giant. How the Japanese Economy Works* (Washington, The Brookings Institu-tion).

[127] Prindle, P. H. (1985) 'Peasant-worker Households and Community

Based Organisations in Rural Japan', *Modern Asian Studies*, 19, part 2 (April).

[128] Ranis, G. (1959) 'The Financing of Japanese Economic Development', *Economic History Review*, 11, no. 3, reprinted in [112].

[129] Ranis, G. (1955) 'The Community-centred Entrepreneur in Japanese Development', *Explorations in Entrepreneurial History*, 8, no. 2 (December).

[130] Reischauer, E. O. and Craig, A. M. (1979) *Japan. Tradition and Transformation* (Sydney).

[131] Richardson, B. M. and Ueda, T. (eds) (1981) *Business and Society in Japan* (New York, Praeger).

[132] Roberts, J. G. (1973) *Mitsui. Three Centuries of Japanese Business* (New York, Weatherhill).

[133] Robins-Mowry, D. (1983) *The Hidden Sun. Women of Modern Japan* (Boulder, Westview Press).

[134] Rosovsky, H. (1961) *Capital Formation in Japan, 1868–1940* (New York, Glencoe).

[135] Rosovsky, H. (ed.) (1966) *Industrialization in Two Systems* (New York and London, Wiley).

[136] Rosovsky, H. (1968) 'Rumbles in the Rice Fields. Professor Nakamura vs. the Official Statistics', *Journal of Economic History*, 27, no. 2 (February).

[137] Rostow, W. W. (1971) *The Stages of Economic Growth* (Cambridge).

[138] Rostow, W. W. (1978) *The World Economy. History and Prospect* (London, Macmillan).

[139] Schumpeter, E. B. *et al.* (1940) *The Industrialisation of Japan and Manchukuo, 1930–1940* (London, Macmillan).

[140] Sheldon, C. D. (1958) *The Rise of the Merchant Class in Tokugawa Japan, 1600–1868* (New York, Augustin).

[141] Shimada, H. (1980) 'The Japanese Employment System', *Japanese Industrial Relations*, Series 6 (Tokyo, Japan Institute of Labour).

[142] Shinohara, M. (1962) *Growth and Cycles in the Japanese Economy* (Tokyo).

[143] Shinohara, M. (1970) 'A Survey of the Japanese Literature in Small Industry', in B. F. Hoselitz, *Structural Changes in Japan's Economic Development* (Tokyo, Kinokuniya).

[144] Shirai, T. (ed.) (1983) *Contemporary Industrial Relations in Japan* (Wisconsin).

[145] Shiveley, D. A. (ed.) (1976) *Tradition and Modernisation in Japanese Culture* (Princeton).

[146] Sievers, S. L. (1983) *Flowers in Salt. The Beginnings of Feminist Consciousness in Modern Japan* (Stanford).

[147] Silberman, B. S. and Harootunian, H. D. (eds) (1974) *Japan in Crisis. Essays on Taisho Democracy* (Princeton).

[148] Sinha, R. P. (1969) 'Unresolved Issues in Japan's Early Economic Development', *Scottish Journal of Political Economy*, 16 no. 2 (June).

[149] Sinha, R. (1982) *Japan's Options for the 1980s* (London, Croom Helm).

[150] Skinner, K. A. (1980) 'Conflict and Command in a Public Japanese Corporation', *Journal of Japanese Studies*, 6, no. 2 (Summer).

[151] Smith, R. J. (1979) 'The Ethnic Japanese in Brazil', *Journal of Japanese Studies*, 5, no. 1 (Winter).

[152] Smith, R. J. (1983) *Japanese Society. Tradition, Self and the Social Order* (Cambridge).

[153] Smith, T. C. (1955) *Political Change and Industrial Development in Japan: Government Enterprise 1868–1880* (Oxford).

[154] Smith, T. C. (1959) *The Agrarian Origins of Modern Japan* (Stanford).

[155] Smith, T. C. (1973) 'Pre-Modern Growth. Japan and the West', *Past and Present*, no. 60 (August).

[156] Smith, T. C. (1977) *Nakahara: Family, Farming and Population in a Japanese Village, 1717–1830* (Stanford).

[157] Sumiya, M. and Taira, K. (eds) (1979) *An Outline of Japanese Economic History. Major Works and Research Findings* (Tokyo).

[158] Tada, H. (ed.) (1980) *A Selected Bibliography on Socio-economic Development of Japan. Part I: circa 1600–1940* (Tokyo, UN University Project Team, Institute of Developing Economies).

[159] Taeuber, I. B. (1958) *The Population of Japan* (Princeton).

[160] Taira, K. (1970) *Economic Development and the Labor Market in Japan* (Columbia).

[161] Taira, K. (1978) 'Factory Labour and the Industrial Revolution in Japan', *Cambridge Economic History of Europe* (Cambridge); vol. VII, part 2.

[162] Thunberg, C. P. (1796) *Voyages au Japon* (Paris, Dandré), vol. III.

[163] Tipton, F. B. (1981) 'Government Policy and Economic Development in Germany and Japan, a Skeptical Revaluation', *Journal of Economic History*, 41, no. 1 (March).

[164] Totman, C. D. (1980) *The Collapse of the Tokugawa Bakufu* (University of Hawaii).

[165] Tsuji, K. (1981) 'Are the Japanese Workaholics?' *Japan Quarterly*, 28, no. 4 (October–December).

[166] Umemura, M. (1979) 'Regional Differences in the Distribution of Industrial Employment in Japan', *The Developing Economies*, 7, no. 2 (June).

[167] Veblen, T. (1934) 'The Opportunity of Japan' in *Essays in Our Changing Order* (New York, Viking).

[168] Vogel, E. F. (1971) *Japan's New Middle Class* (Berkeley).

[169] Vogel, E. F. (1979) *Japan as Number One. Lessons for America* (Harvard).
[170] de Vos, G. A. and Wetherall, W. O. (1974) *Japan's Minorities. Burakumin, Koreans and Ainu* (London, Minority Rights Group).
[171] Waswo, A. (1977) *Japanese Landlords: The Decline of a Rural Elite* (Berkeley).
[172] Williamson, J. G. (1965) 'Regional Inequality and the Process of National Development', *Economic Development and Cultural Change*, 13, no. 4, part 2 (July).
[173] Williamson, H. G. and de Beuer, L. J. (1978) 'Saving, Accumulation and Modern Economic Growth', *Journal of Japanese Studies*, 4, no. 1 (Winter).
[174] Yamaguchi, M. and Kennedy, G. (1984) 'Contribution of Population Growth to per capita Income and Sectoral Output Growth in Japan, 1880–1970', *The Developing Economies*, 22, no. 3 (September).
[175] Yamamura, K. (1968) 'A Re-examination of Entrepreneurship in Meiji Japan (1868–1912)', *Economic History Review*, 21, no. 1 (April).
[176] Yamamura, K. (1977) 'Success Illgotten? The Role of Meiji Militarism in Japan's Technological Progress', *Journal of Economic History*, 36, no. 1 (March).
[177] Yamamura, K. (1974) *A Study of Samurai Income and Entrepreneurship* (Harvard).
[178] Yamamura, K. (1978) 'Entrepreneurship, Ownership, and Management in Japan', in *Cambridge Economic History of Europe* (Cambridge), vol. VII, part 2.
[179] Yamamura, K. *et al.* (1985) 'Symposium on *ie* Society', *Journal of Japanese Studies*, 11, no. 1 (Winter).
[180] Yonekawa, S. (1985) 'Recent Writings on Japanese Social and Economic History', *Economic History Review*, 38, no. 1 (February).

Bibliographical update

Since the first edition, decelerating growth, recession, financial upheavals, political instability and the emergence of Asiatic competitors have focused more attention on 'whither Japan?' [61, 67] rather than on 'how Japan did it?' None the less, economic history continues to elicit an increasing literature in Japanese [72] and in other languages. Some of the important English language works are noted here and others are listed in bibliographies [3, 53, 56, 68].

The *Cambridge Encyclopedia of Japan* [8] provides a comprehensive, scholarly introduction. There is much more detail, with extensive references, many in Japanese, in the *Cambridge History of Japan* [12, 23, 34]. Macpherson's book [40] in a series on Industrial Revolutions has an introductory overview, a reading list of 1,000 items and a collection of 21 essays by distinguished Western and Japanese scholars from Crawcour to Yamamura. Economic development is the theme of Francks [17] and Ohkawa and Kohama [50], and Minami has both a quantitative analysis of Japan with international contrasts [41] and one of China with Japanese comparisons [42]. The three-volume *Political Economy of Japan* [32, 37, 73] mainly deals with post-World War II and is a splendid successor to Patrick's and Rosovsky's *Asia's New Giant*. Revisionist views on the roots of modern industrialisation are in Fischer *et al.* [16], and Latham and Kawakatsu [38] look for preconditions in centuries of Asian trade with China at the centre. The 'Marxist' interpretation, no longer dominant in Japanese historiography, is discussed in Albritton [1], Hoston [27] and Morris-Suzuki [47]. These and scrutinies of minorities [63, 64] and protest [6, 7] are a salutary reminder that the benefits of 'capitalist' development did not trickle down to all groups. Women's studies are burgeoning [5, 33, 39, 48, 62], Hanley [25] has a symposium on gender and Hunter [30] and her contributors not only review the conditions and wages of females in coalmining, diving and domestic service but give insights into their motives and the perception of their role as employees and mothers.

Further light has been thrown on the Tokugawa era by Howell on proto-industrialisation [28] and by Feeney's and Hameno's statistical exercise on fertility and rice prices [15]. Essential reading on the transition from Tokugawa to Meiji is in Jansen and Rozman [35] which includes Akira Hayami on demography and Yamamura on the land tax. That doyen of Western Japanologists, T. C. Smith, has gathered 10 of his articles, for example on pre-modern growth, population control and merit as ideology [57]. The socio-cultural, economic and political antecedents of modern Japan are explored in a translation by Nakane and Oishi [49] containing, inter alia, studies on agriculture and rural industry, urban networks, the *Bakuhan* system and the practices of family business which evolved into Japanese-style management.

In the 'modern' period the role of the State remains controversial and the complexities are difficult to evaluate in a short pamphlet. The euphoria about 'Japan Inc.' since World War II has been qualified [51, 66]. For pre-war there are many references in the general works, Garon [19] looks at labour and Samuels at energy and national security [54, 55]. The last is closely related to international trade, well covered by Yamazawa [74]. On foreign business Yuzawa and Udagawa [76] edit one of the numerous 'proceedings' of the Fuji Conferences. Grabowski [21, 22] continues to produce papers on agriculture and all aspects of this topic with plenty of statistics are in the indispensable Hayami and Yamada [26]. Labour and industrial relations are the focus of Gordon [20] and Kinsley [36] offers a cynical appraisal of 'harmony'.

Management practices, the envy of the West, are addressed by one of the Fuji Conferences [75] and by Wray [69]. Wray [70], Fukasaku [18] and Chida and Davies [10] have histories of shipping and shipbuilding and Erickson's [14] is one of the few sources on railways. Although the origins of modern growth may be uncovered in pre-industrial years, the impact of Western technology remained a *sine qua non*. Checkland [9] assesses the British influence, Westney [65] highlights imitation of Western organisations, Otsuka *et al.* [52] analyse factor endowments and choice of technique in Indian and Japanese textiles, and there is a number of investigations into the acquiring and adaptation of foreign technology [13, 31, 43, 46]. The relative neglect of banking history is corrected by Tamaki [59] and the rise of Nomura, now supreme in world finance, is documented by Alletzhauzer [2].

Although there may be no adequate substitute for a knowledge of the Japanese language, English readers are fortunate in the proliferation of accessible books. In addition many Japanese journals now have English versions. These are at once elucidating interpretation of Japan's past and spawning new controversies. How reliable, for example, is the data base for so much quantitative research, the L.T.E.S. of Ohkawa *et al.*? How relevant is the 'new' institutional methodology? In what sense was Japan unique [11]? What were the costs and benefits of militarism and imperialism? And, judging by British experience, we are only on the threshold of the 'standard of living' issue. There remain not only plenty of lacunae in our historical knowledge but also endless prospects for the ahistorical, cliometric counter-factualist.

Updated bibliography

[1] Albritton, R. (1991) *A Japanese Approach to Stages of Capitalist Development*. Basingstoke: Macmillan.

[2] Alletzhauser, A. L. (1990) *The House of Nomura: the Rise to Supremacy of the World's Most Powerful Company*. London: Bloomsbury.

[3] Asada, S. (ed.) (1989) *Japan and the World, 1853–1952: a Bibliographic Guide to Japanese Scholarship in Foreign Relations*. New York: Columbia University Press.

[4] Beasley, W. G. (1990) *The Rise of Modern Japan*. London: Weidenfeld and Nicolson.

[5] Bernstein, G. L. (ed.) (1991) *Recreating Japanese Women, 1600–1945*. Berkeley and Los Angeles: University of California Press.

[6] Bix, H. D. (1986) *Peasant Protest in Japan*. New Haven: Yale University Press.

[7] Bowen, R. W. (1988) 'Japanese Peasants: Moral, Rational, Revolutionary, Duped'. *Journal of Asian Studies*, 47 (November), pp. 821–32.

[8] Bowring, R. and Kornicki, P. (1993) *The Cambridge Encyclopedia of Japan*. Cambridge: Cambridge University Press.

[9] Checkland, O. (1989) *Britain's Encounter with Japan, 1868–1912*. Basingstoke: Macmillan.

[10] Chida, T. and Davies, P. N. (1990) *The Japanese Shipping and Shipbuilding Industries: a History of their Modern Growth*. London: Athlone.

[11] Dale, P. N. (1986) *The Myth of Japanese Uniqueness*. London: Croom Helm.

[12] Duus, P. (ed.) (1988) *The Cambridge History of Japan*, vol. VI. *The Twentieth Century*. Cambridge: Cambridge University Press.

[13] Thomas-Emeagwali, G. (1991) 'Technological Transfer: Explaining the Japanese Success Story'. *Journal of Contemporary Asia*, 21, pp. 504–12.

[14] Erickson, S. J. (1985) *State and Private Enterprise: Railroad Development in Meiji Japan*. Ann Arbor: University Microfilms International.

[15] Feeney, G. and Hameno, K. (1990) 'Rice Price Fluctuations and Fertility in Late Tokugawa Japan', *Journal of Japanese Studies*, 16 (Winter).

[16] Fischer, W., McInnes, R. M. and Schneider, J. (eds) (1986) *The Emergence of a World Economy*. Weisbaden: Verlag.

[17] Francks, P. (1992) *Japanese Economic Development: Theory and Practice*. London: Routledge.

[18] Fukasaku, Y. (1993) *Technological and Industrial Development in Prewar Japan: Mitsubishi Nagasaki Shipyard, 1884–1934*. London: Routledge.

[19] Garon, S. M. (1992) *The State and Labor in Modern Japan*. Berkeley and Los Angeles: University of California Press.

[20] Gordon, A. (1985) *Evolution of Labor Relations in Modern Japan*. Cambridge, Mass.: Harvard University Press.

[21] Grabowski, R. (1991) 'Economic Development and the Traditional Sector: A Comparison of Japanese and African Experience'. *The Developing Economies*, 29 (March), pp. 3–18.

[22] Grabowski, R. and Paskura, C. (1988) 'Technical Efficiency in Japanese Agriculture'. *The Developing Economies*, 26 (June), pp. 172–86.

[23] Hall, J. W. (ed.) (1991) *The Cambridge History of Japan*, vol. IV. *Early Modern Japan*. Cambridge: Cambridge University Press.

[24] Hane, M. (1986) *Modern Japan: a Historical Survey*. Boulder and London: Westview Press.

[25] Hanley, S. B. *et al.* (1993) 'Symposium on Gender and Women in Japan'. *Journal of Japanese Studies*, 19 (Winter), pp. 1–120.

[26] Hayami, Y. and Yamada, S. (1991) *The Agricultural Development of Japan: a Century's Perspective*. Tokyo: University of Tokyo Press.

[27] Hoston, G. A. (1986) *Marxism and the Crisis of Development in Pre-War Japan*. Princeton: Princeton University Press.

[28] Howell, D. L. (1992) 'Proto-industrial Origins of Japanese Capitalism'. *Journal of Asian Studies*, 51 (May), pp. 269–86.

[29] Hunter, J. E. (1989) *The Emergence of Modern Japan: an Introductory History since 1853*. London: Longman.

[30] Hunter, J. E. (ed.) (1993) *Japanese Working Women.* London: Routledge.

[31] Inkster, I. (1990) *Transferred Development: Western Technology and Industrialisation of Japan*. London: Kegan Paul.

[32] Inoguchi, T. and Okimoto, D. I. (eds) (1988) *The Political Economy of Japan*, vol. II. *The Changing International Context*. Stanford: Stanford University Press.

[33] Iwao, S. (1993) *The Japanese Woman: Traditional Image and Changing Reality*. New York: The Free Press.

[34] Jansen, M. B. (ed.) (1989) *The Cambridge History of Japan*, vol. V. *The Nineteenth Century*. Cambridge: Cambridge University Press.

[35] Jansen, M. B. and Rozman, G. (eds) (1986) *Japan in Transition: from Tokugawa to Meiji*. Princeton: Princeton University Press.

[36] Kinsley, W. D. (1991) *Industrial Harmony in Modern Japan: the Invention of a Tradition*. London: Routledge.

[37] Kumon, S. and Rosovsky, H. (eds) (1992) *The Political Economy of Japan*, vol. III. *Cultural and Social Dynamics*. Stanford: Stanford University Press.

[38] Latham, A. J. H. and Kawakatsu, H. (eds) (1994) *Japanese Industrialisation and the Asian Economy*. London: Routledge.

[39] Lebra, T. S. (1984) *Japanese Women, Constraint and Fulfilment*. Honolulu: University of Hawaii Press.

[40] Macpherson, W. J. (ed.) (1994) *The Industrialization of Japan*. Oxford: Blackwell.

[41] Minami, R. (1994) *The Economic Development of Japan: a Quantitative Study*. Basingstoke: Macmillan, 2nd edn.

[42] Minami, R. (1994) *The Economic Development of China: a Comparison with the Japanese Experience*. Basingstoke: Macmillan.

[43] Minami, R., Kim, K. S., Makino, F. and Seo, J. H. (1995) *Acquiring, Adapting and Developing Technologies: Lessons from the Japanese Experience*. Basingstoke: Macmillan.

[44] Molony, B. (1991) *Technology and Industrialisation: the Pre-war Chemical Industry*. Cambridge, Mass.: Harvard University Press.

[45] Morikawa, H. (1992) *The Rise and Fall of Family Enterprize Groups in Japan*. Tokyo: University of Tokyo Press.

[46] Morris-Suzuki, T. (1994) *The Technological Transfer of Japan from the Seventeenth to the Twenty First Centuries*. Cambridge: Cambridge University Press.

[47] Morris-Suzuki, T. and Seiyama, T. (eds) (1989) *Japanese Capitalism since 1945*. Armonk, N.Y. and London: M. E. Sharpe.

[48] Nakamura, N. (ed.) (1994) *Technological Change and Female Labor in Japan*. Tokyo: United Nations University Press.

[49] Nakane, C. and Oishi, S. (eds) (1990) *Tokugawa Japan: the Social and Economic Antecedents of Modern Japan*. Tokyo: University of Tokyo Press.

[50] Ohkawa, K. and Kohama, H. (1989) *Lectures on Developing Economies: Japan's Experience and its Relevance*. Tokyo: University of Tokyo Press.

[51] Okimoto, D. I. (1989) *Between MITI and the Market*. Stanford: Stanford University Press.

[52] Otsuka, K., Ranis, G. and Saxonhouse, G. (1988) *Comparative Technological Choice in Development: the Indian and Japanese Cotton Textile Industries*. New York: St Martin's Press.

[53] Perren, R. (1992) *Japanese Studies from Prehistory to 1990: a Bibliographical Guide*. Manchester: Manchester University Press.

[54] Samuels, R. J. (1987) *The Business of the Japanese State: Energy Markets in Comparative and Historical Perspective.* Ithaca and London: Cornell University Press.

[55] Samuels, R. J. (1994) *Rich Nation, Strong Army: National Security and the Technological Transformation in Japan.* Ithaca and London: Cornell University Press.

[56] Shulman, F. J. (1990) *Japan. World Bibliographical Series,* vol. 103. Oxford: Clio Press.

[57] Smith, T. C. (1988) *Native Sources of Japanese Industrialisation, 1750–1920.* Berkeley and Los Angeles: University of California Press.

[58] Sugiyama, C. (1994) *Origins of Economic Thought in Modern Japan.* London: Routledge.

[59] Tamaki, N. (1995) *Japanese Banking: a History, 1859–1959.* Cambridge: Cambridge University Press.

[60] Totman, C. (1993) *Early Modern Japan:* Berkeley and Los Angeles: University of California Press.

[61] Tsuru, S. (1994) *Japan's Capitalism: Creative Defeat and Beyond,* Cambridge: Cambridge University Press.

[62] Tsurumi, E. P. (1990) *Factory Girls: Women in the Thread Mills of Meiji Japan.* Princeton: Princeton University Press.

[63] de Vos, G. A. (1992) *Social Cohesion and Alienation: Minorities in the United States and Japan.* Boulder: Westview Press.

[64] Weiner, M. (1989) *The Origins of the Korean Community in Japan.* Atlantic Highlands, N.J.: Humanities Press International.

[65] Westney, D. E. (1987) *Imitation and Innovation: Transfer of Western Organisational Patterns to Japan.* Cambridge, Mass.: Harvard University Press.

[66] Wood, C. (1994) *The End of Japan Inc. and How the New Japan Will Look.* New York: Simon and Schuster.

[67] Woronoff, J. (1990) *Japan as Anything but Number One.* Basingstoke: Macmillan.

[68] Wray, W. D. (ed.) (1989) *Japan's Economy: a Bibliography of its Past and Present.* New York: Wiener.

[69] Wray, W. D. (ed.) (1989) *Managing Industrial Enterprize: Cases from Japan's Prewar Experience.* Cambridge, Mass.: Harvard University Press.

[70] Wray, W. D. (1985) *Mitsubishi and the N.Y.K., 1870–1914: Business Strategy in the Japanese Shipping Industry.* Cambridge, Mass.: Harvard University Press.

[71] Yamamoto, H. (1993) *Technical Innovation and the Development of Transportation in Japan.* Tokyo: United Nations University Press.

[72] Yamamura, K. (ed.) (1991) 'Review of Nihon Keizai-shi: Japanese New Economic History Writings'. *Journal of Japanese Studies,* 17 (Winter), pp. 127–42.

[73] Yamamura, K. and Yasuba, Y. (eds) (1987) *The Political Economy of Japan,* vol. I. *The Domestic Economy.* Stanford: Stanford University Press.
[74] Yamazawa, I. (1990) *Economic Development and International Trade: The Japanese Model.* Honolulu: University of Hawaii Press.
[75] Yui, T. and Nakagawa, K. (eds) (1989) *Japanese Management in Historical Perspective.* Tokyo: Proceedings of the Fifteenth Fuji Conference, University of Tokyo Press.
[76] Yuzawa, T. and Udagawa, M. (eds) (1990) *Foreign Business in Japan Before World War II.* Tokyo: Proceedings of the Sixteenth Fuji Conference, University of Tokyo Press.

Index

New Studies in Economic and Social History

Previously published as

Studies in Economic History

Titles in the series available from the Macmillan Press Limited

Economic History Society

The Economic History Society, which numbers around 3,000 members, publishes the *Economic History Review* four times a year (free to members) and holds an annual conference.

Enquiries about membership should be addressed to

The Assistant Secretary
Economic History Society
PO Box 70
Kingswood
Bristol
BS15 5TB

Full-time students may join at special rates.